DYNASTIES
of
DEVOTION

DYNASTIES
of
DEVOTION

DEEPA MANDLIK

Translated from the Marathi by
ABOLI MANDLIK

HarperCollins *Publishers* India

First published in English in India by HarperCollins *Publishers* 2025
4th Floor, Tower A, Building No. 10, DLF Cyber City,
DLF Phase II, Gurugram, Haryana – 122002
www.harpercollins.co.in

2 4 6 8 10 9 7 5 3 1

First published in Marathi as *Parakrami Hindu Rajanchi Advitiya Mandire* by Rajendra Prakashan 2022

Copyright © Deepa Mandlik 2025
Translation copyright ©Aboli Mandlik 2025

P-ISBN: 978-93-6569-653-0
E-ISBN: 978-93-6569-708-7

The views and opinions expressed in this book are the author's own and the facts are as reported by her, and the publishers are not in any way liable for the same.

Deepa Mandlik asserts the moral right to be identified as the author of this work.

All rights reserved. No part of this publication may be reproduced, stored in a retrieval system, or transmitted, in any form or by any means, electronic, mechanical, photocopying, recording or otherwise, without the prior permission of the publishers.

Typeset in 11.5/16 Adobe Garamond Pro at
HarperCollins *Publishers* India

Printed and bound at
Thomson Press (India) Ltd.

This book is produced from independently certified FSC® paper to ensure responsible forest management.

A unique legacy forged through heroic achievements,
Passed down into our care,
Igniting the flame of pride within our hearts,
To those who bestowed fortune upon us,
To the countless unnamed contributors ...

With heartfelt gratitude and deep reverence.

CONTENTS

	Translator's Note	ix
	Foreword	xi
	Preface	xvii
1.	Sculpting Divinity: Exploring the Mysteries of Kailasa Temple	1
2.	The Creator of Kailasa	25
3.	A King's Grand Dream: The Brihadeeswara Temple	41
4.	The Iconic Brihadeeswara Temple at Gangaikondacholapuram	65
5.	Timeless Beauty: The Art and History of Airavatesvara Temple	83
6.	Tracing the Ancient Echoes of Hindu Culture in Cambodia	103
7.	A Veritable Repository of Art: The Chennakeshava Temple	129
8.	Delving into the Mystery of the Sree Padmanabhaswamy Temple	151
	Glossary	171
	Acknowledgements	183

TRANSLATOR'S NOTE

As the translator of this remarkable exploration into the intricacies of temples and their profound cultural significance, I am honoured to present to you the translated edition of my mother's book, a labour of love that delves into the rich tapestry of history, art and spirituality woven by ancient temples.

Growing up, I witnessed my mother's passion for travelling and her insatiable curiosity about temples and their history. Her journey, chronicled in the original Marathi text, has now been extended to a wider audience through this translation. It has been my privilege to render her words into English, allowing readers beyond the original audience to partake in this celebration of Indian heritage.

This book is not just a mere exploration of temples; it is an odyssey that traverses countries, from the sacred shrines in south India to the awe-inspiring Angkor Wat in Cambodia. The temples and sculptures discussed here are not only architectural marvels but also symbols of cultural exchange and spiritual unity.

TRANSLATOR'S NOTE

As a translator, my endeavour has been to capture the essence of my mother's prose, ensuring that the beauty and depth of her words resonate with readers in the translated form. The information about each temple, each sculpture, and every historical detail has been carefully translated to preserve the authenticity and passion that my mother poured into her writing.

I am deeply grateful to her for entrusting me with this significant task, and I extend my gratitude to the readers for embarking on this literary journey. May this translated edition offer you the same sense of wonder, enlightenment and awe that the original text has imparted to its readers.

Aboli Mandlik

FOREWORD

Upon receiving the book *Dynasties of Devotion* written by Deepa Mandlik, I was immediately intrigued by its title, as it suggested something new and noteworthy. As I delved into its pages, I realized I was right. The book sets out the narratives of seven temples—each a testament to the noble kings who, through their vision and valour, brought these architectural marvels to life. In the hands of the author, the bravery of these kings is not just acknowledged but gloriously celebrated.

What stands out in the narrative is the author's commitment to providing readers with credible information. As the historical tales of these kings' valour unfold, the author grapples with a delicate decision—whether to place special emphasis on the temple architecture or not. Admirably, Deepa Mandlik has successfully navigated this dilemma, ensuring that both aspects receive due and appropriate attention throughout the narrative.

Temples and sculptures are distinctive features of Indian culture. Temples have been built since ancient times across civilizations in present-day countries such as Egypt, Italy, Greece, Iraq, Iran, and beyond. A notable example is the temple housed in the Metropolitan Museum of Art in New York, discovered during the excavation of the Aswan Dam. Museums like the National Museum of Iran in Tehran and the Vatican Museums in Rome also showcase ancient sculptures, attesting to the global significance of these cultural treasures. In India, there is an abundance of temples, adorned with sculptures of deities who are worshipped, instead of being housed in museums. The sheer variety of sculptures can be overwhelming for researchers.

This book is a detailed and scholarly exploration of iconic temples like the Kailasa Temple in Ellora, the Brihadeeswara Temple in Thanjavur and Gangaikondacholapuram, the Airavatesvara Temple in Darasuram, and the Chennakeshava Temple in Belur. The historical context of these temple constructions is presented with meticulous care, prompting readers to ponder whether the author is a history scholar or an expert in temple architecture.

Among the numerous temples outside India, the author has chosen to focus specifically on temples in Cambodia. This deliberate selection stems from the fact that the temple here is not only the creation of the mighty King Suryavarman-II but is also currently the largest Vishnu temple in the world, inspired by Indian culture. Whether in India or Cambodia, the author's meticulousness and aesthetic sense is evident in the thoughtful curation of temples.

Typically, the study of temples tends to overlook the historical background of their creation. However, author Deepa Mandlik addresses this gap by providing detailed historical contexts. Examining the history of ancient India reveals a pattern wherein ambitious kings of various dynasties constructed magnificent temples in or near the capital city to honour their deities. Professor Anant Sadashiv Altekar, a scholar in the history of these dynasties, notes that it was because the capital of the Rashtrakuta dynasty was situated near Shulabhanjan, close to the town of Ellora, that Krishnaraj-I, a formidable ruler of this dynasty, built the monolithic Kailasa Temple at Ellora. A similar historical perspective can be applied to other temples discussed in this book.

In the first chapter, the author provides a comprehensive understanding of Kailasa and its creator. The question of the temple's creator is addressed in two places in the book. The author dismisses speculations suggesting alien involvement in the creation of Kailasa, highlighting the importance of grounding interpretations in historical context. The author's keen ability to observe and appreciate the beauty of craftsmanship is most evident in her depiction of 'Kalyanasundara murti' and 'Ravananugraha murti'.

The curious tourist in the author is evident in her distinctive writing style. Unlike temple scholars who may focus on intricate historical aspects, Deepa's approach caters more to the needs of tourists. In essence, she takes a mixed approach, embodying elements of both a scholar and a tourist. This duality becomes apparent in her descriptions, such as the account of accessing the Brihadeeswara Temple in Thanjavur and the anticipation felt before entering the Gangaikondacholapuram Temple. The selection of both these temples for the book reflects the author's discerning choices, and her writing style possesses the unique ability to convey the soulful essence of the temples' sculptures to readers.

Throughout her writings, Deepa Mandlik seamlessly integrates references to folktales and mythologies. However, what distinguishes her work is the careful balance she maintains, ensuring that these do not overshadow the objective depiction of the temples' history and the appreciation of the sculptures. For instance, she acknowledges that Karuvurar Devar was referred to as the guru of King Rajaraja of the Chola dynasty, but aptly notes the absence of evidence connecting the king and the guru, who are mentioned separately in the inscriptions. Additionally, Deepa dispels misconceptions, such as the notion that the Gangaikondacholapuram Temple is a mere replica of the Thanjavur Temple. Through astute observation, she intricately compares the placement of shikharas and establishes the architectural differences between the two.

The writer's ability to observe and describe the beauty of nature is vividly apparent in her introduction to the Airavatesvara Temple in Darasuram. As she delves into the sculptures of this temple, her writing becomes more sophisticated, capturing the intricacies of the small sculptures on the columns with a compelling narrative. A highlight lies in her close observation of the detailed sculptures, particularly in the discussion of Parvati engaging in penance between three consecutive columns, leading to her marriage with Shiva (Kalyanasundara murti) and the subsequent portrayal of the panigrahan ritual. Interestingly, Parvati, the daughter of Himavan and Mena, represents jiva (living being). Her union with Shiva through marriage or the panigrahan ceremony symbolizes the spiritual oneness of jiva and Shiva (God).

The Chennakeshava Temple in Belur, Karnataka, is lauded as a 'veritable repository of art' by the author. Her detailed exploration captures various facets of the temple: its art, religious significance, and the distinctive contributions of its artists. Drawing a delightful analogy, she likens the experience of a visit to the temple to a satisfying meal of puranpoli (a Maharashtrian delicacy), leaving one content and fulfilled.

The author pays special attention to the forty-eight pillars in the temple's assembly hall, where each pillar is distinct. Notably, she describes the Narasimha column and challenges conventional beliefs by stating that it could be rotated, contrary to the assertions made by Kamalika Bose and noted temple scholar George Mitchell in their book *The Hoysala Legacy: Belur, Halebidu, Somanathapura*. Examining the research done in this regard, I agree with the view expressed by the author.

In the book, the description of Sree Padmanabhaswamy Temple in Thiruvananthapuram, India follows that of Angkor Wat, located outside India. Temples and idols serve as symbols of India's vibrant culture spreading to Southeast Asia through peaceful means. It has left an enduring influence that is still prominent in Cambodia (ancient Kamboj). The Angkor Wat temple symbol holds a place of prominence on the national flag and currency notes of Cambodia. It is recognized as the largest temple in the world and is known as Vishnu Lok. The author, after an eight-day stay in Cambodia, extensively covers temples such as Angkor Thom, and Bayon, among others, providing a compelling narrative that should be read thoroughly.

The author's sense of wonder and her persistence is evident in her chapter on Padmanabhaswamy Temple. Her remarkable ability to unravel mysteries, including the revelation of the priceless wealth stored there, is a highlight of the book. I would encourage readers to read the chapter to see the mystery unfold.

This book possesses the power to keep readers engaged from start to finish. With a determined approach, the author has embarked on a journey to various temples, reading numerous reference books along the way. Through her hard work, she has successfully completed this book. Vinod Mandlik, Deepa's husband, credited for most of the photographs in the book, contributes significantly to its visual appeal. I hope that a second edition of this book will soon be released, enhanced by the feedback of curious readers.

Dr G.B. Deglurkar
Former vice-chancellor, Deccan College
(Deemed University), Pune

PREFACE

Namaskar,

I am delighted to present to you the book *Dynasties of Devotion*. Travelling has been an integral part of my life, as my husband Vinod, and I have a special interest in exploring ancient temples. Over the years, we have visited numerous temples, yet it was our visit to the Sree Padmanabhaswamy Temple in Kerala that sparked a newfound passion for research and writing.

The allure of the treasure in the temple's underground chambers, shrouded in mystery and surrounded by myriad beliefs, motivated me to comprehensively research it. Although I gathered substantial information from various sources, I did not come across any detailed articles covering all the facets of the temple. Driven to close this gap, I meticulously researched and wrote an exhaustive article. This piece was then submitted to the esteemed editor Shri Anand Antarkar for review and later accepted for publication in the *Naval* Diwali issue.

The response from readers was overwhelmingly positive, with calls and emails expressing appreciation and a desire to revisit the temple with a fresh perspective. The positive reception of the article and the genuine need for such information being made available inspired me to continue my writing journey. Emboldened by this encouragement, during the Diwali vacations of the same year, we explored several ancient temples in Cambodia. We witnessed the grandeur of the largest temple dedicated to Lord Vishnu, along with other Hindu and Buddhist temples. Additionally, the onset of Hindu culture in that country seemed very fascinating to me and inspired me to author the article 'Tracing the Roots of Hinduism in Cambodia'.

Our travels also took us to Tamil Nadu, where we marvelled at three temples considered to be the finest examples of Dravidian architecture. These temples, known as the 'Great Living Chola Temples', built by the visionary Chola kings, became the focus of subsequent articles. The rich art and history of the Chola dynasty compelled me to research further, sparking a series of articles chronicling their courage and vision.

The journey of my book found its roots in the pages of *Naval* Diwali issues, where my articles, 'Tracing the Roots of Hinduism in Cambodia' and 'A King's Grand Dream: Brihadeeswara Temple of Thanjavur', found a home in subsequent years. I received the insightful guidance of Shri Anand Antarkar during this journey. Unfortunately, he is no longer with us but his wisdom, encouragement and support remain eternally with me. I am also indebted to my guru, senior writer Madhavitai Kunte, whose constant encouragement and testimonies became wellsprings of inspiration for my subsequent articles.

My vision for this book was not for it to be merely a travelogue, but to convey the essence of temple architecture, its unique features, its historical background, the mythological stories associated with these temples and the inspiration behind their construction.

While these temples are immensely important from a religious and cultural viewpoint, the visionary kings who dedicated themselves to constructing and preserving these marvels are equally vital. Usually, while visiting ancient temples, great importance is placed on the temple deity. Amidst the immortal and magnificent structures, the historical narratives of the kings who orchestrated their construction often fade into obscurity. While history buffs, researchers, and scholars may possess this knowledge, this rich history of valour remains less accessible to the wider audience. It is my sincere endeavour that this book will serve to bridge that gap, offering a gateway for readers to discover the captivating histories of these temples and the remarkable rulers who shaped them.

This book gives a glimpse into the captivating histories of the Chola dynasty in south India, the Khmer dynasty in Cambodia, the Hoysala dynasty in Karnataka, the Rashtrakuta dynasty in Maharashtra, and the Cher dynasty in Kerala. While researching the lives of these kings and their dynasties, I was awestruck by their greatness and felt a boundless sense of pride in being connected to such a vibrant culture. If readers can experience even a fraction of these sentiments, I would consider the objective of this book fulfilled.

In my exploration, I drew inspiration from a few noteworthy books that guided me beyond the confines of mere travelogues to incorporate historical backgrounds. Notably, Dr G.B. Deglurkar's *Prachin Bharat: Etihas ani Sanskruti* stands out. Dr Deglurkar is a scholar of history, iconography, and an authority on archaeology. His book provided a fresh perspective on Indian history, shedding light on the insufficient recognition our mighty kings and rich culture often receive. Simultaneously, S.L. Bhairappa's history-rich literary works, such as *Sarth*, depicting the eighth century, and *Avaran*, spanning the history before and after Independence, further fuelled my desire to infuse historical depth into my articles.

These temples, holding much historical and cultural significance, should be known as the identity of India. The architectural design, grandeur, creativity and engineering of these temples are remarkably advanced. Moreover, emphasis must be laid on the fact that they were not only built as places of worship but were also instrumental in the overall societal and economic development of the times. Particularly in the south, these grand temples served as hubs for art, culture, trade, politics and social welfare. These multi-purpose temples were an important source of employment during those times. Notably, while these temples are dedicated to various deities, they reflect the architectural influences of Shaivism, Vaishnavism, Buddhism and Jainism. The secularism evident in sculptural art is an indicator of the progressive societal development of that era.

Our culture and the history created by our great rulers can be an intimidatingly vast subject. This book earnestly endeavours to present this rich history in an engaging manner, making it accessible to readers. My sincere attempt is to convey the true essence of the subject, with the hope that it will reach as many people as possible.

As mentioned earlier, the esteemed Dr G.B. Deglurkar has been a guiding light, inspiring me to infuse historical context into my writings. His extensive work in this domain has not only provided valuable guidance but has also introduced me to the profound depth of this subject. It was a sincere yearning of mine for this book to bear his foreword, and I was elated when he graciously agreed, sparing time from his busy schedule to review this work. I consider myself truly fortunate to have received his valuable guidance and support.

I express my heartfelt gratitude to Smt. Neelima Kulkarni from Rajendra Publications, who, even during the challenging times of the COVID-19 pandemic, took on the responsibility of publishing the original text in Marathi. She worked tirelessly on this project with unwavering enthusiasm and optimism. I am deeply indebted to her for her invaluable support.

A special acknowledgement goes to my husband, Vinod Mandlik, who has been my #1 supporter. Without his efforts, this book would have remained a distant dream. I sincerely hope that this book reaches a wide audience and contributes to preserving the legacy of our ancestors' achievements and progressive culture in the minds of readers.

Deepa Mandlik

1

SCULPTING DIVINITY: EXPLORING THE MYSTERIES OF KAILASA TEMPLE

The Kailasa Cave Temple, located thirty kilometres from Aurangabad at Ellora, is very close to my heart. Growing up in Aurangabad, over the years, I had made multiple visits to the culturally rich sites of Ellora, Ajanta, Devagiri, Grishneshwar and Paithan—all in close proximity. Trips to these historical wonders were guaranteed any time guests would visit. Just as children do not truly appreciate their parents until later in life, I realized the significance of the Kailasa Temple and the brilliance of its creators much later on. After I had visited numerous historical sites around the world, it dawned on me that none of them could hold a candle to the sheer grandeur and beauty of the Kailasa Temple. This realization sparked a newfound eagerness to revisit the temple and perceive it in a fresh light. Seizing the opportunity of a long weekend, my husband and I flew down to Aurangabad and headed to Ellora at dawn the next day.

While the sun shone brightly during our journey from Aurangabad to Ellora, the chill of dawn lingered in the air. The scenic landscapes initially visible from the windows of our car gradually disappeared as we drove on. Closer to Kailasa Temple, I felt the excitement one feels when visiting a loved one after years. Universally acknowledged to be a site with incomparable craftsmanship, the Kailasa Cave Temple was erected in the eighth century by the kings of the Rashtrakuta dynasty. The Ellora Caves (which house the Kailasa Temple in Cave No. 16) were designated a UNESCO World Heritage site in 1983.

The practice of cave construction in India can be traced back to the second century BCE, during the reign of the Satavahana dynasty. These caves, strategically placed along trading routes, served as crucial waystations. With the rapid spread of Buddhism, there was a growing requirement to house Buddhist monks during their varshavas (rains retreat). Varshavas refers to the rainy months during which Buddhist monks take shelter in one place. This demand fuelled the construction of caves for the monks' varshavas.

Following the rule of the Satavahana dynasty, present-day Maharashtra was successively ruled by the Vakataka dynasty, Chalukya dynasty and Rashtrakuta dynasty. Each dynasty continued the practice of constructing caves and emerged as generous patrons of the arts. This historical continuity is a key factor explaining why, out of the 1,200 caves in India, more than 1,000 are found in Maharashtra.

Upon stepping out of the car at Ellora, we found ourselves amidst the bustling energy of hundreds of tourists who, like us, had chosen to spend their long weekend exploring the Ellora Caves. After procuring our tickets from the ticket counter with some difficulty, owing to the long line, we made a beeline towards Cave No. 16 without paying much heed to the many hawkers selling beautiful necklaces, caps and water bottles.

The sprawling garden in front of the Kailasa Temple lined with bountiful crowned neem trees and flower bushes added a lively contrast to the surrounding black stone mountains. Out of the thirty-four caves in Ellora, twelve are Buddhist caves, seventeen are Hindu caves and five are Jain caves. These were constructed over the centuries by different ruling dynasties owing to diverse religious influences. A majority of these caves were constructed between the sixth to the eighth century. It is impossible to see all the caves in one day, especially if one seeks to appreciate the unique beauty of each one. Consequently, most tourists only visit a certain number of caves. Cave No. 16 (Kailasa Temple) is a favourite, celebrated for its unparalleled architecture. The Kailasa Temple is the only cave-temple in the world of its size to be vertically excavated. Carvers started work at the peak of the rock and carefully excavated downward. One cannot begin to imagine the sheer scale, planning and rigid implementation required to carve the temple from the crest down to its last step with the precise strokes of a chisel. While sculptures or columns carved from a single rock are deemed remarkable, the Kailasa Temple takes this to the next level, as the entire structure is hewn from a single basalt rock.

Strolling along the path next to the garden, we reached the entrance of Cave No. 16. Although the architecture has a Dravidian influence, the gopura (entrance door) is unique and has a distinct style. The gopura is two-storeyed. Despite being a Shiva temple, the Kailasa Temple is not strictly Shaivite, which is clear from the gopura itself, adorned with massive sculptures of different avatars of Shiva (on the left) and Vishnu (on the right). Unfortunately, most of these sculptures have weathered with time. Looking at the sculptures of the Ashta Dikpalas (group of eight deities ruling over the eight quarters of the Universe), along with their mounts, made me curious about the wonders inside the temple. Upon entering, one is greeted by depictions of the rivers Ganga and Yamuna, personified as women on either side of the door. These rivers, which are symbols of holiness and devotion in Hinduism, seemingly serve as a reminder to keep a pure mind while stepping into the temple. Progressing through the corridor, a colossal sculpture of Ganesh on the left wall blesses the temple's construction, wishing good fortune upon all who enter. On the right wall stands a sculpture of Mahishasurmardini (Goddess Kali)—its placement near the entrance perhaps intended to ward off those with malicious intentions towards the temple. As we reached the end of the corridor, my gaze fixed upon a mesmerizing sight that held me captive. Before us stood a magnificent and grand sculpture of Gajlakshmi (Goddess Lakshmi). As the crowd surrounding the sculpture dispersed, I hurried closer to witness the sculpture in its full glory—the lotus leaves crowding the bottom half of the sculpture, Goddess Lakshmi elegantly sitting on the lotus emerging from the leaves, surrounded by four elephants, two on each side with one above the other. The elephants in the bottom were filling up pots with water and the ones above were showering the goddess with the water. The Gajalakshmi is a symbolic representation of the rains (the elephants) showering the earth (Goddess Lakshmi) with water. It felt like a proclamation of prosperity by the Rashtrakutas right at the temple's entrance.

THE MIGHTY RASHTRAKUTA DYNASTY

The Rashtrakuta dynasty, a formidable force that reigned for approximately 225 years, held sway over the entirety of India for a significant period. A closer examination of this heroic dynasty, originating in Maharashtra, unveils a legacy marked by wealth, prosperity and stability. Intriguingly, the term 'Rashtrakuta' did not initially denote rulers but functioned as a title, much like Deshmukh or Desai. Inscriptions from the Rashtrakuta era claim their origin from Lord Krishna or his military commander, Satyaki, although there is no historical evidence supporting these assertions.

Eminent historian V.V. Mirashi suggests that the Rashtrakutas comprised three clans—the Manpur clan from Man, Satara district; the Nandivardhan clan from Achalpur, Vidarbha; and the Verul (Ellora) clan from Marathwada.[1] A copper inscription from the Rashtrakuta dynasty refers to Verul as 'Elapur'. Verul was known

---

1 P.G. Sahastrabuddhe, *Maharashtra Sanskruti* (Continental Prakashan, 1979), p.130.

as Elapur since it was situated on the banks of the Ela river, from which the English name Ellora was derived. The Rashtrakuta clan from Elapur would later become emperors and establish their own dynasty. The other clans were not as successful. The founder of the Verul clan is considered to be Dantidurga, who was an official for the Chalukyas of Gujarat. Later, as the Chalukyas lost power, Dantidurga seized the opportunity to establish independent rule. During his reign, Dantidurga conquered the territories of Laat (south Gujarat), Maharashtra, Vidarbha and also invaded the far-off kingdoms of Kosal (Chhattisgarh), Kalinga (Odisha) and Srisailam. Dantidurga's successor, Krishnaraj-I, ended the reign of the Chalukyas and solidified Rashtrakuta's dominance. During his eighteen-year reign, Krishnaraj-I tripled the size of the kingdom by conquering Karnataka, Vengi (of the Eastern Chalukyas), Andhra Pradesh and Konkan. In this manner, Krishnaraj-I laid a firm foundation for the future growth of the Rashtrakuta dynasty. The renowned Kailasa Temple is believed to have been built during Krishnaraj-I's rule. Krishnaraj-I's successors continued his mighty and valiant legacy. The Rashtrakuta dynasty ruled from 750 CE to 973 CE, asserting its dominance over all of India, with the exception of Punjab and Sindh. Numerous Rashtrakuta copper plate inscriptions have been unearthed in south Maharashtra. According to some researchers, many of Krishnaraj-I's successors may have contributed to the construction of the Kailasa Temple.

 The structure of this Kailasa Temple constructed by the Rashtrakutas is quite captivating. The temple is ninety-one metres long, over thirty metres tall, and has a width of fifty-three metres. The temple is surrounded by a horseshoe-shaped courtyard. On two sides of the courtyard, there are two life-size elephant sculptures and two flagpoles. While these unique flagpoles are still in good condition, unfortunately, the same cannot be said about the elephant sculptures. The design of the Kailasa Temple is inspired by the Kailasa mountain, the celestial abode of Shiva. Placed in the middle of the courtyard, the temple mirrors the structure of the Kailasa mountain, with the main shrine of the temple on the first floor, similar to how Shiva resides on the peak of the Kailasa mountain. Connected to the main temple is a Nandi mandapa (a pavilion of the sacred bull Nandi), linked by a stone bridge. On the opposite side, another stone bridge connects the Nandi mandapa to the gopura.

The bottom-most layer of the temple is gilded with exquisitely carved large elephants. These carvings lend the impression that these elephants bear the weight of the temple. The earlier mentioned horseshoe-shaped courtyard surrounding the temple is lined with alcoves enclosed by columns. The symmetrical columns lining the alcoves and the various views of the temple afforded by the alcoves are simply marvellous. One cannot help but be impressed by the architectural and engineering skills used at the time: the immaculate craftsmanship of the sculptures leaves one spellbound.

However, the real creator of this beautiful temple remains a subject of debate. While some consider Krishnaraj-I as the creator of the temple, conflicting views persist due to the absence of inscriptions in the temple premises recording this. A copper plate inscription from the time of King Karka-II, who ruled from 972 CE to 991 CE, found at Vadodara, Gujarat, credits Krishnaraj-I with building a Shiva temple at Elapur. The copper plate tells an amusing story of the time when the gods were travelling in their plane over Elapur and were amazed by the incredible temple built by Krishnaraj-I. The gods remarked that the temple could not possibly be man-made. The sculptor who made the temple was even more stunned by the temple and exclaimed, 'This is unbelievable, I do not know how I built this.' In this manner, the copper plate sings poetic praises of the temple.

Similarly, in the later generation of Rashtrakutas, Akalvarsha Krishna-III's copper plate inscription also gives credit for the construction of the temple to a king named Krishnaraj. However, it is unclear which King Krishnaraj the inscription refers to since it is devoid of details of the time of his reign. According to some, the temple was constructed by the founder, Dantidurga, and completed by his successor, Krishnaraj-I, who ruled from 756 CE to 773 CE. Cave No. 15 of the Ellora Caves was built during Dantidurga's rule, which is documented in a stone inscription. Curious to see this inscription, we made sure to climb up and visit Cave No. 15. The inscription is carved on the wall of a small mandapa and is not very clear. The inscription, consisting of fourteen lines and 29.5 shlokas (verses), records the genealogy of the Rashtrakutas and that King Dantidurga had visited the temple premises along with his army. We saw many sculptures that were similar to those in Cave No. 16, but in better condition. The sculptures are beautiful and intricate, however, they appear to be earlier attempts at achieving perfection, because the craftsmanship of the sculptures at Kailasa Temple is far superior. According to certain sources, the work of Cave No. 15 started by Dantidurga was also completed by Krishnaraj-I, which might explain the similarities between the two. There is no information on the time taken to complete the construction of the Kailasa Temple, but it is believed that the major part of the construction took eighteen years, which was done during Krishnaraj-I's rule. While historian M.K. Dhavalikar supports this view, he also believes that the installation of certain important sculptures and other construction was undertaken by Krishnaraj-I's successors. Considering this view, the temple may have taken over 100 years to reach its final form.

SCULPTURAL SPLENDOUR IN THE ALCOVES

The alcoves in the temple host massive sculptures of various Hindu deities. Despite being tempted to, I have refrained from elaborating on each sculpture since there is enough to write about them to fill an entire book. Therefore, let us focus on some of the important sculptures at the Kailasa Temple. A special characteristic of these sculptures carved in the eighth century is that they are grand and life-size, sometimes even larger than life. In the alcoves on the left, one finds the rivers Saraswati, Yamuna and Ganga depicted as women. The sculptures of the deities are surrounded by decorative vines and flanked on either side by makara toranas (decorative arches with crocodile motifs). The deities are each on their mounts—Yamuna on a tortoise, Ganga on a crocodile and Saraswati on a lotus flower.

After moving further ahead and climbing up the stairs, one finds the Lankeshwar Hall. The Nataraj sculpture in the hall is intricately carved. However, insufficient lighting hinders the visibility of the other sculptures. As you progress further down the line of alcoves, rows of sculpted panels unfold. Many of these are based on tales of Shiva from the Puranas. The panels depict the tales beautifully, capturing the essence of the story. The experience is much more enjoyable if one knows the tales before viewing these sculptures. The faces of the sculptures are very expressive. One of the alcoves on the left showcases a sculpture of Shiva and Parvati playing chaupar (a strategic board game). The sculpture is divided into two panels. It beautifully portrays the playful relationship of Shiva–Parvati. In

The front facade of Kailasa Temple, Maharashtra

Kailasa Temple from the photo point

The view from the alcoves of the Kailasa Temple adorned with sculpted elephants

The Saptamatrikas (the shakti forms of Gods) who aided Shiva in slaying the demon Andhakasur at Kailasa Temple

A beautiful Gajalakshmi sculpture—a symbolic representation of the earth (Goddess Lakshmi) being showered by rainwater (the elephants), associated with wealth and prosperity—at Kailasa Temple

Shiva and Parvati seated gracefully on an intricately carved Nandi, with the joyful and chubby Ganas depicted at the bottom of the sculpture at Kailasa Temple

Depiction of the Ramayana on the walls of Kailasa Temple

The famous sculpture of Kailasutthan which gives the Kailasa Temple its name

the middle of the panel, Shiva–Parvati are sitting across each other with the chaupar board between them, with Shiva's mischievous expression giving away that he is cheating and Parvati appearing frustrated at his tactics. Parvati's right leg is slightly lifted, showing her in the middle of her attempt to leave the game. Shiva is trying to stop Parvati from leaving with one hand and asking for one more game with another. The sculpture is so beautiful that it feels like this couple is, in fact, in front of the viewer. The lower part of the panel portrays Parvati's friend trying to reign in Nandi, the bull, whom Parvati had won in the first game and Shiva's ganas (attendants) obstructing her. Nandi, in particular, is very finely carved.

These sculptures convey the emotions of the persons depicted in the scene through their body language. The kalyanasundara Shiva–Parvati sculpture depicting their marriage is a prime example. The sculpture shows the pair during panigrahan (a marital ritual during which the groom typically takes the hand of the bride), when Parvati takes the hand of Shiva, instead of the converse. According to the story in the Puranas, Shiva was unwilling to marry. However, due to Parvati's dedicated penance, and immense persuasion by the gods due to the need for Kartikeya (Shiva and Parvati's first born) to come into the world and defeat the monster Tarakasura, Shiva agrees to the marriage. This may be the reason for depicting Parvati as the one taking charge and taking Shiva's hand into her own. While she does that, she is still bashful (as was idealized in women at the time), which is evident from her neck being slightly lowered, her other hand toying with the cloth covering her front and her left toe scratching her leg. I was amazed by the astute observational skills of the sculptor.

Another expressive sculpture portrays Ravana's devotion towards Shiva. It depicts the story of when the gods hid the lotus flowers to be offered for the Shivalinga pooja, leading Ravana to cut off nine of his ten heads and offer them instead, in order to complete the pooja. Another version of this story relates that in order to please Shiva, Ravana began his penance and would cut off one of his heads every thousand years and offer it to Shiva. After offering nine heads, when it was time to cut off the last head, Shiva appeared before him and granted him a boon. The sculpture depicting this scene is beautifully carved. The nine cut-off heads of Ravana do not express any pain and, in fact, appear satisfied and honoured that they have been sacrificed to Shiva. This type of sculpture is only seen in three places in Maharashtra—the Kailasa Temple, the Aundha Nagnath Temple in Hingoli, and the Markanda Temple in Gadchiroli.

The next sculpted panel depicting Markandeyanugrah is also one that cannot be missed. The story behind the sculpture goes as follows: Saint Markand, a great devotee of Shiva, fervently desired a son. He prayed to Shiva for a son and his wish was granted; however, his son was cursed to die young. The son, Markandeya, was very intelligent and also a devotee of Shiva. The sculpture tells the tale of young Markandeya praying to Shiva, when Yamaraj (the god of death) tries to take him away. Shiva is enraged by the attempt to kill his devotee and appears from the Shivalinga and gives Yamaraj a brutal kick in the stomach. Yamaraj is taken aback by Shiva's appearance and prays for forgiveness. This avatar of Shiva is known as Kalaari or Kalantak [kaal (time) + antak (ender)] since he defeats Yamaraj, who is seen as a symbol of time. This sculpture, showing Shiva's grace and his rage, appears both in the alcoves and on the main shrine's wall.

Another sculpted panel, Lingodbhava, which is a manifestation of Lord Shiva emerging from a linga, is seen in the alcoves positioned exactly opposite the middle of the main shrine. This type of sculpture is found on the wall behind the main shrine in many south Indian temples. The story behind the sculpture is one where Vishnu and Brahma were having an argument over which of the two is superior, when suddenly a jyotirlinga (pillar of light) appeared. The two decide that the one who finds where the pillar begins or where it ends will be deemed superior. In order to investigate, Vishnu assumes the form of a varaha (boar) and descends to patal (the underworld) to find the end, and Brahma takes the form of a swan and ascends to the sky to find the beginning. Unable to find the end of the pillar despite his efforts, Vishnu concedes defeat. However, Brahma deceitfully declares his success by bringing ketki flowers and lying that they had been offered upon the peak of the pillar. At this moment, Shiva manifests from the middle of the pillar, leading Vishnu and Brahma to accept his superiority and bow down to him. Enraged at Brahma's lie, Shiva curses him, declaring that he will not be worshipped by anyone anywhere. The story showcases Shiva's omnipresence and superiority, explaining why this sculpture is placed at the centre of the sanctum sanctorum. The composition of the sculpture is interesting: it features Shiva in the middle of the jyotirlinga, next to him a full-sized Vishnu with the varaha avatar near his feet, descending into hell, a four-headed Brahma and above him the swan flying skyward. This grand sculpture can also be seen on the front wall of the main shrine.

Another important sculpture in the alcoves is the Atmalinga (soul of Shiva). Pleased by Ravana's devotion, Shiva gives him the atmalinga and warns him not to place it on the ground during his journey. Ganesha cleverly tricks Ravana and places the atmalinga on the ground. The sculpture brilliantly captures Ravana's frustration and efforts to pick up the atmalinga, which is growing taller and taller at the place where it touches the ground. It is said that the place where the atmalinga touched the ground is Gokarna Mahabaleshwar, in Karnataka, where one can find a temple dedicated to it. Apart from sculptures featuring stories of Shiva, the alcoves also feature sculptures of Vishnu, such as the slaying of Hiranyakashipu, the Varaha avatar, Trivikrama, Sheshashayi Vishnu and Annapurna. The sculpted panel of Kaaliyamardan, depicting Krishna (an avatar of Vishnu) slaying Kaaliya (the snake) is particularly memorable.

THE LEGEND ASSOCIATED WITH KAILASA TEMPLE

While we were in the alcoves, it had become quite sunny outside. The crowd of tourists seemed to have increased. From the alcoves, the elephant carvings on the lower part of the temple, illuminated by the sun, were a treat to look at. Stepping down from the alcoves, our attention was drawn to the uncarved portion of the hulking mountain that towered above us, without any external support. The pillars of the alcoves are an astonishing twenty feet inside from the outer end of the looming mountain. I craned my neck and admired this chisel-marked roof for a long time, wondering how the sculptors carved this incredible monolithic temple from the peak of the mountain.

Delving into the architectural technicalities of the temple, there is a difference of opinion among experts. Instead of dwelling on these differences, let me share a fascinating legend about what led to this temple being carved vertically, from the peak to the base. This story is found in the book *Kathakal Pataru*, written by Krishna Yajnavalki (1470 CE to 1535 CE).

According to this story, the king who ruled over this region fell gravely ill. In a desperate plea for the king's recovery, the queen made a navas (solemn vow) to Shiva, pledging to construct a Shiva temple and refrain from consuming any food until she laid eyes on the shikhara (peak) of the temple. As fate would have it, the king gradually regained his health, prompting the initiation of plans for the temple to fulfil the queen's sacred vow. Eager to expedite the temple's construction, the king invited multiple architects. However, all of them said that the temple would require several months to be built. At this point, an architect named Kokas approached the king with a bold promise—to reveal the shikhara of the temple within a matter of weeks. Selecting the Charanadri mountain range for this ambitious endeavour, Kokas commenced is work on Mount Mahishadri. Employing an ingenious approach, Kokas decided to carve down the mountain vertically, presenting a solution that defied the conventional construction methods. He kept his promise to the queen by unveiling the shikhara within the specified timeframe. Witnessing the completion of the shikhara, the queen was able to break her fast, marking the fulfilment of her vow.

According to eminent historian M.K. Dhavalikar, the Kailasa Temple was, in fact, designed by the architect Kokas, who was known as Manikeshwar. Kokas hailed from an illustrious family, and it is suggested that the Kailasa Temple may have been named Manikeshwar after him. Until the eighteenth century, the Kailasa Temple might have been known as Manikeshwar as indicated by a stone inscription from the time of Ahilyabai Holkar (1725 CE to 1795 CE). The inscription records her efforts to restore and maintain the temple and refers to the temple as Manikeshwar. Traces of the painting work undertaken as part of the restoration can still be seen today. While there is clear evidence that this temple was formerly called Manikeshwar, there is a conflict of opinion about who it is named after. Some believe that the story about the queen who made the navas, while slightly different from the legend, is based on true events. They suggest that the name of the temple, Manikeshwar, comes from this queen, i.e., Krishnaraj-I's queen Manikawati. Enamoured by the Kailasanath Temple at Kanchipuram built by the Pallavas, she wished that Krishnaraj-I would also build a temple. Since there was a delay in building the temple, she vowed to fast until she saw the shikhara of the temple, which is why the temple was built through vertical excavation.

While the exact origin of the name Manikeshwar remains unclear, a few points are noteworthy. First, there may be some credence to the story about the queen's wish to build a temple after seeing the Kailasanath Temple at Kanchipuram. Scholars acknowledge that the temple architecture and sculptures at the Kailasa Temple show influences of Chalukya and Pallava styles. The Kailasa Temple is particularly thought to be inspired by the Pallavas' Kailasanath Temple at Kanchipuram and the Chalukyas' Virupaksha Temple at Pattadakal. While the Kailasa Temple has drawn inspiration from these other temples, it is undeniable that the Rashtrakutas have built a unique and extraordinary cultural monument. The history behind the Chalukya and Pallava influence is quite interesting. The Chalukyas and Pallavas were bitter rivals due to which at least one war would erupt in every generation. The Chalukya king Vikramaditya-II, who ruled from 733 CE to 745 CE, defeated the Pallavas in one such war. To commemorate this victory over the Pallavas' capital Kanchipuram, the Virupaksha Temple at Pattadakal was constructed, inspired by the Kailasanath Temple at Kanchipuram. The work on the Virupaksha Temple was undertaken by the same sculptors who had made the Kailasanath Temple. Later, when the Rashtrakutas defeated the Chalukyas, they, in turn, drew inspiration from the Virupaksha Temple and built the Kailasa Temple at Ellora. Experts believe that the same sculptors who built the Virupaksha Temple and Kailasanath Temple were engaged for the construction of the Kailasa Temple, owing to the similarity in architectural style.

The second noteworthy point is that the sculpture of Queen Manikawati found in the yajnashala hall (place where sacrifices are made to the sacred fire), further south in the alcoves also reinforces the theory of her being the person after whom this temple was named. The yajnashala hall contains an artful scene of hom-havan (offerings made to a sacred fire), where Queen Manikawati is portrayed as the host, flanked by two attendants fanning her and the Saptamatrikas (group of seven Hindu goddesses). Despite the deterioration of many of these sculptures, the surviving parts provide a glimpse into the original beauty and artistry in making them. It is very rare to find Saptamatrikas sculptures of this scale and detail. The tales of the Saptamatrikas can be found in the Puranas. According to the Mahabharata, King Prahlad, a devotee of Vishnu, was succeeded by the evil King Andhakasur, who tortured his subjects and led the kingdom to descend into chaos. King Andhakasur had received a boon from Brahma that if anyone tried to kill him, a new Andhakasur would emerge from every drop of his blood. The boon had made him fearless, and no one dared to stop him. The gods requested Shiva to defeat this evil king. Knowing the arduous task Shiva was faced with, the gods sent their shakti (power) female forms, the Saptamatrikas, to support him. With the assistance of the Saptamatrikas, Shiva vanquished the evil Andhakasur. In another version of this story, Andhakasur was smitten by Shiva's wife Parvati. When he came to take Parvati away, Shiva killed him with the help of the Saptamatrikas. While the sculptures of the Saptamatrikas in the Kailasa Temple are not in optimal condition, one can find better preserved representations in Cave No. 14 (Ravana ki Khai),

Cave No. 15 (Dashavatar) and Cave No. 21 (Rameshwar). The Saptamatrikas, being the shakti form of the gods, are depicted with each god's mount and symbols, which makes them recognizable. They are: Brahma's shakti, Brahmani with a swan; Maheshwar's shakti, Maheshwari with a bull; Kartikeya's shakti, Kaumari with a peacock; Vishnu's shakti, Vaishnavi with an eagle; Varaha's shakti, Varahi with a boar; Indra's shakti, Indrani with Airavata (the divine elephant); and Yama's shakti, Chamunda with a man/corpse. It is typical for sculptures of the Saptamatrikas to also feature Ganesh and Virbhadra playing the veena.

SCULPTURES OF THE MAIN TEMPLE

The sculptures at the Kailasa Temple are predominantly female. The Rashtrakutas have showcased their reverence for women by featuring the sculptures of women: the symbols of purity, Ganga–Yamuna near the entrance; two distinct sculpted panels of the murderous Mahishasurmardini; symbol of prosperity Gajalakshmi; independent hall containing Ganga, Yamuna and Saraswati depicted as women; symbol of lust Rati; Annapurna; and the yajnashala hall's Saptamatrikas along with Rani Manikawati. The story of the birth of the Saptamatrikas and the defeat of Andhakasur is also found at the Kailasa Temple. In this sculpture, the Saptamatrikas are shown in miniature form near the right foot of Shiva. Regrettably, the heads of the Saptamatrikas have been severed, owing to foreign invasions.

Descending the stairs of the yajnashala, the countless sculptures of the main temple clamoured for attention. The sculptures portraying scenes from the Ramayana and Mahabharata stood out, unique due to their miniature size. These panels capture the gist of the story while featuring the major characters and events. The lengthy Mahabharata has been condensed into merely five panels and the Ramayana into eight panels. Another special feature of these panels is their very intentional location in this west-facing temple. The Mahabharata panels are on the left wall of the temple, which faces north, since the events in the Mahabharata took place in north India. Similarly, the Ramayana panels are on the right wall, which faces the south, since the events took place in south India. The thoughtful arrangement reflects the consideration behind each sculpture and gives a glimpse into the historical and geographical proficiency of ancient Hindus. The Mahabharata panels show different scenes—the birth of Krishna, him enjoying nature, the slaying of the evil Kamsa and several scenes of the Mahabharata war. One of the most expressive sculptures is that of the weaponless and chariot-less Abhimanyu fighting off warriors using the wheel of his broken chariot. Another notable sculpture is Arjunanugraha, which portrays pashupatastra (a celestial missile) being given by Shiva to Arjun as a reward for passing the test set by Shiva. The Ramayana panels are equally finely carved and expressive. Scenes such as Rama's banishment, the hunt of the kanchanmruga (illusional golden deer), Sita's abduction, Sita spending time at Ashoka vatika, the war between Vali and Sugreeva, and Lanka being set on fire, are shown. One is instantly captivated by the exquisite artistry of the panels.

The most lauded sculpture at Kailasa Temple is that of Ravananugraha or Kailasutthan. Since the subject depicted is very popular, it is seen in many temples, although structured differently. While the Airavateswara Temple at Darasuram and Chennakeshwar Temple at Bellur have beautiful Kailasutthan sculptures, the one at Kailasa Temple brilliantly depicts the expressions of each character in the scene. It is said that this sculpture was carved a few years after the construction of the temple and gives the temple its name as

Kailasa Temple. The Kailasutthan sculpture narrates a Puranic story wherein after defeating his stepbrother Kuber, Ravana, a devotee of Shiva, set out to meet Shiva on Mount Kailasa. However, since Shiva and Parvati were in the middle of an intense fight, the guards did not let Ravana climb the mountain. Ravana was enraged by the guards denying him entry. Arrogant about his strength, he attempted to lift Mount Kailasa. The manner in which the scene is depicted speaks volumes about the sculptor's knowledge of human psychology. It is amusing to observe the reactions of the residents of the mountain to the intense tremors caused by Ravana's actions. Ravana is shown on one knee, using all his strength to lift the mountain. His head is tilted to one side due to the heavy weight, with the earring on that side touching his shoulder. Parvati is shown gripping Shiva's arm tightly. Her attendant is shown turned away, running in fright. The monkeys in the trees and Shiva's ganas attendants are also portrayed in a state of disarray. The ganas are shown hurling giant boulders at Ravana. Shiva is shown calmly exerting pressure on his toe to bury Ravana in the ground. Two of his guards, sitting on either side of Shiva, are also shown to be composed—confident in Shiva's strength. The upper part of the panel depicts sages along with their wives, eager to watch the crushing of Ravana's ego. This remarkable sculpture is a must-see for every visitor.

After seeing the wonderful sculptures of Mahashivayogi, Gajasuravadha, Natarajashiva and others, we headed to see the famous Tripurantakashiva sculpture. This sculpture is again based on a tale from the Puranas. In the story, Tarakasur (the monster for whose defeat the gods convinced Shiva to get married) had three sons—Vidyunmali, Tarakaksh and Kamalaksh—who pray to Brahma to attain immortality and receive a boon. According to the boon, each son is granted a floating city in the sky made of gold, silver and iron, respectively. These cities align in a row every thousand years, and the sons can only be defeated if all three cities are destroyed in one shot. The boon makes the evil trio even more boisterous, and they start wreaking havoc on earth. The sculpture portrays the moment when Shiva goes on his chariot to defeat them. Notably, this is the only story in the Puranas in which Shiva uses his chariot. The chariot is driven by Brahma; the wheels are Surya (sun) and Chandra (moon); Shiva's bow is made of the four vedas; the bowstring is Savitri; and the arrow is of Agni, Yama and Vishnu. To convey a sense of speed, the sculptors have cleverly used a corner spot on the walls (two panels at a right angle from each other), presenting Shiva holding the bow and Brahma steering the chariot on one wall, while the other wall showcases the galloping horses pulling the chariot. This piece is an excellent indicator of the incredible architectural and sculptural knowledge of the sculptors of the time.

THE MAIN TEMPLE

Evading the growing crowd, we ventured into the main temple on the first floor. The mandapa welcomed us with its sixteen finely carved pillars, adorned with depictions of gods, goddesses, scenes from the Puranas, and even erotic sculptures. These pillars are decorated with arches and vines, reminiscent of the sculptures at Ajanta. It brings to mind an intriguing anecdote I once read about the Vakatakas, the rulers preceding the Rashtrakutas. The Vakatakas had a large part to play in the construction of the caves at Ajanta. According to the eminent historian Arvind Jamkhedkar, the last Vakataka ruler King Harishena's rule was one of advancements in the field of art, sculpture and architecture. However, after his death, at the end of the fifth century, the construction work at Ajanta halted. Legend has it that the hundreds of artisans working at Ajanta migrated to Ellora to sustain themselves, under the wing of the newly established Rashtrakuta dynasty. The stylization of the art at Ajanta and Ellora seems to suggest that this theory is true, particularly when one looks at the other caves at Ellora.

Our attention then shifted to the gilded ceiling of the mandapa, where stunning paintings from the Rashtrakuta era are, astonishingly, still visible. The mandapa, formerly known as Rangamahal, is decorated with vibrant paintings on the ceiling and artful sculptures, which surely must have been a spectacle to behold when they were freshly made. The painting of Nrityashiva (dancing Shiva) seems to follow you with its eyes wherever you go. The sculpture of Nrityashiva and Parvati on the ceiling is exquisitely carved. Unfortunately, due to the lack of necessary lighting, one cannot fully appreciate the beauty of the art in the mandapa. Ahead of the sanctum sanctorum, there are two sculptures of Shiva–Parvati facing each other: one in decent condition and one significantly damaged. Within the sanctum sanctorum, a massive Shivalinga dominates the space, occupying the entire area with just enough room for one person to stand beside it. According to a copperplate inscription found at Baroda, the Shivalinga in the Kailasa Temple was studded with jewels during Krishnaraj-I's time. However, today, since the Shivalinga is not worshipped, nary a flower is offered to it.

After taking darshan, we exited the temple through the door to the left of the sanctum sanctorum. In the open space surrounding the main temple, there are five small beautifully decorated temples. While there are no sculptures of deities inside the small temples, these little temples are adorned with fine carvings. The first of these small temples has two erotic sculptures on either side of the door on the front-facing wall. According to the author of *Bharatiya Shilpavaibhav*, Dr S.R. Deshpande, experts say that this temple must be of Kamadeva (the Hindu god of love and desire). In the other small temples and the main temple, the outer walls of the main shrines are decorated with ornate sculptures of Shiva, in different forms. These grand sculptures, dispersed around the upper part of the temple without any background scenery, create the illusion of them floating in the sky. Our gazes lingered on these sculptures on the lower part of the outer walls for a long time.

We then proceeded to the Nandi mandapa. We marvelled at the carvings of the short, plump ganas above the entrance. We entered the mandapa while admiring these and the erotic sculptures on the lower section of the outer wall. The sculpture of Nandi had deteriorated over time. We moved to the next mandapa after seeing the flagpoles from the windows of the Nandi mandapa. Both ends of this mandapa are flanked by galleries, which are now popular photo points. From the elevated vantage of the gallery, one can see the Nandi mandapa, the bridge, the main temple, the shikhara of the temple and the sculptures decorating it, the flagpoles and the giant sculptures of elephants, the alcoves and finally, the hulking mountain out of which this temple has been carved. It is natural that such a gorgeous scene results in droves of tourists vying to get their photos clicked. Waiting for the crowd to thin, I tried to absorb as much of the beautiful scenery as possible. While doing so, I reflected on the incredible contributions of the Satavahanas, Vakatakas, Chalukyas and Rashtrakutas to this monument. Their governance and bravery gave this place the necessary stability and prosperity to foster the flourishing of art, sculpture and craft. At the same time, the thought of the destruction of the monument caused by invasions made me feel disheartened. As soon as we had the opportunity, we clicked photographs to our hearts' content.

Ascending the mountain next to the road near the temple exit offers a unique perspective of the entire temple premises. Although the climb is a bit cumbersome, it is worth the glorious view that one gets to enjoy. Gazing at this spectacle, one cannot help but think of the incredible feat achieved by the sculptors and architects of the time, who vertically excavated this remarkable and unparalleled monolithic temple. It made me reflect on the greatness of my ancestors and instilled a sense of pride in me, for having descended from such accomplished individuals.

2
THE CREATOR OF KAILASA

The Kailasa Temple stands as a global icon, renowned for its distinctive architecture and unparalleled artistry. Constructed in the eighth century, nearly 1,200 years ago, this grand cave-temple is a monumental feat, hewn from a monolithic mountain rock. It proudly holds the title of the world's largest cave-temple. The identity of its creator remains a subject of curiosity. While some historical evidence sheds light on this enigma, there is a lack of extensive and tangible proof such as the stone inscriptions found in ancient south Indian temples, leaving room for speculation as to the temple's construction.

There are multiple theories floating around the creation of the Kailasa Temple on various mediums, with social media taking the lead. A plethora of theories based on inconsistent and unreliable information is spread on social media authoritatively without any supportive proof. This proliferation has led to widespread misinformation. In the course of my research, I encountered diverse perspectives on this intriguing subject.

Due to the extraordinary nature of Kailasa Temple, some people have formulated a strange conspiracy theory positing that it was not the work of humans but a creation of aliens with the help of advanced technology. The arguments supporting this peculiar theory are, undoubtedly, entertaining to peruse. Notably, among the thirty-four caves at Ellora, where Kailasa resides, this notion of alien involvement is attached only to this one cave. The question arises: why is this alien logic selectively applied to Kailasa, and what underpins the scepticism towards the accomplishments of ancient Hindus?

The prevalence of such theories, divorced from historical evidence and facts—and circulating rapidly in video form on social media—

is disheartening. There is an abundance of historical evidence at our disposal, which is sufficient to debunk this unfounded theory. It remains imperative to delve into the rich history of the state of Maharashtra from ancient times to do so. Acquiring knowledge of this historical backdrop unveils the understanding of how a remarkable structure like the Kailasa cave could be crafted in this land. This chapter aims to provide an overview of Maharashtra's history and disprove the alien theory surrounding the Kailasa Temple.

RULERS OF ANCIENT MAHARASHTRA

In the context of Maharashtra, the term 'ancient period' encompasses the era until the thirteenth century. During this period, the state was ruled predominantly by the Satavahanas, Vakatakas, Chalukyas, Rashtrakutas and Yadavas. We will focus on the history of Maharashtra until the tenth century, a period marked by the reign of the Rashtrakutas, under whose auspices the Kailasa Temple was built. Throughout history, the creation of art and culture has thrived in societies marked by prosperity and affluence. The flourishing of the arts requires political and social stability, and the preservation of these cultural expressions relies heavily on a secure environment. Security plays a pivotal role as it enables the conservation of heritage, providing a tangible link to the past and allowing us to trace history.

While learning about the leaders who ruled Maharashtra in ancient times, these facts become more pronounced. Foremost among them is the successful defence against foreign invasions, a feat that eluded the powerful northern states of India. Maharashtra's rulers prevented foreign invaders from setting foot on their soil, ensuring the safety of south India from external threats. This defence strategy safeguarded the region's religion and culture, fostering their preservation and development. Additionally, the ambitious rulers of these dynasties established enduring power in the region. As a result, people experienced good governance, prosperity and cultural growth. This chapter examines evidence of such prosperity through the lens of the Kailasa Temple in Ellora, a testament to the flourishing art and culture during this historical period.

The recorded history of Maharashtra begins with the Satavahana dynasty, known as Shalivahan in Sanskrit and Salihan in Prakrit, before the Common Era. This dynasty finds mention in the Puranas. Simuka (Srimukh) is considered to be the first king of the Satavahana dynasty. At the time of Ashoka's death around 232 BCE, the Satavahanas were in the process of consolidating their authority in Pratishthan Nagari (present-day Paithan).

In order to get a complete picture of the Indian political landscape at the time, it is important to understand the events transpiring in the rest of India prior to the Satavahana dynasty coming into power. Let us begin with discussing the great conqueror Chandragupta Maurya and his achievements. Chandragupta successfully vanquished the Greek rulers who had established dominance over the northwestern frontier following Alexander's invasion. His resilience against foreign invaders was evident when, facing a formidable challenge, he thwarted the Greek general Seleucus and demoralized the Greek forces at the border. Chandragupta's crowning achievement lay in being the first ruler to unite the entirety of India under his empire.

Subsequently, the next king, King Bindusara, maintained control over this vast kingdom during his reign. However, a significant shift occurred with the ascension of King Ashoka. Exerting his influence as king, Ashoka propagated Buddhism, a religion characterized by non-violence, compassion, renunciation and nihilism. This shift weakened the robust state apparatus established by Chandragupta, providing an opening for Greek invasions over the next 100–150 years. In the absence of resistance from north India, the Greek army effortlessly penetrated the country, conquering territories as far inland as Ayodhya.

In the wake of these events, India faced further challenges with cruel raids by the nomadic tribes of the Sakas and Kushanas. Despite the ensuing turmoil, the prevailing principles of non-violence within society deterred any inclination to resist or engage in combat. The prioritization of achieving enlightenment through religion or dhamma, considered superior to triumph in warfare, allowed invaders to occupy the land swiftly.

During this transitional period, the Satavahana kingdom in the south had attained the status of an empire. The rule of Shri (Sri) Satakarni (194 BCE to 185 BCE)[2] was flourishing. Determined to revive the Vedic religion, he began to expand his empire. Advancing towards the north, he drove out the Sakas from the western Malwa, Ujjain region, and claimed dominion over it. Additionally, he conquered portions of the Narmada and Vidarbha regions from the weakened Mauryan empire. At a time when India was largely Buddhist, Satakarani's commitment to the revival of the Vedic religion is considered his most significant achievement by Hindus. Inscriptions reveal that despite his short reign of only eleven years, he performed the Ashwamedha yajna (fire ritual) twice and the Rajasuya yajna (consecration ritual) once. These actions underscore his dedication to expanding the kingdom and reviving Vedic practices.

---

2 P.G. Sahastrabuddhe, *Maharashtra Sanskruti* (Continental Prakashan, 1979), p. 91.

Another notable Satavahana ruler, Gautamiputra Satakarni (who reigned from 72 to 95 CE or, according to some, 60 to 85 CE), emerged as one of the most distinguished kings of the Satavahana clan. During his time, the brutal, barbaric Sakas had conquered northern India and were making inroads in the south. Gautamiputra decisively defeated the powerful Nahapana and his son-in-law Ushavadat (Rishabhadatta) of the Kshatrapas. He also exiled the Sakas, Greeks, and Pallavas of the south to the north. For this feat, the inscription mentions him as 'Saka Yavana Pallava Nisudana' (The defeater of Sakas, Greeks and Pallavas). Subsequently, Gautamiputra redirected his efforts northwards, liberating Lata (the ancient name for Gujarat) and Maval. His victory led to the inception of the 'Salivahana Saka' calendar, commemorating the defeat of Nahapana. Although the origins of the calendar are debated, it is still in use today. Gautamiputra earned the title 'Trisamudratoyapitavahana' (one whose horses drank the waters of the three oceans/seas) due to the vast expansion of his empire over all of south India and three northern states, reaching the Arabian Sea, the Indian Ocean and the Bay of Bengal. The subsequent Satavahana kings, including Vashishtiputra, Pulumavi, and Sriyagya Satakarni, continued to safeguard the south, preventing the Sakas from setting foot in the region.

The Satavahana dynasty holds profound significance as the first imperial family to the south of the Vindhyas, a region traditionally overshadowed in historical narratives. While ancient texts like the Ramayana and Mahabharata primarily focus on achievements in north India, and legends such as Manu, Yajnavalkya, Panini, Patanjali' Buddha, and Mahavir all hail from the north of India, the Satavahanas emerge as pioneers in shaping the history and culture of south India. Notably, the excavation of caves commenced during the Satavahana period around the second century BCE. The term leni (cave) is believed to have first appeared in an inscription near Nashik's Pandava leni, dating back to the Satavahana era. The inscription also mentions King Krishna, brother of founder King Simuka, as the second Satavahana ruler. From then on, carving work in the Vindhyas and Sahyadri mountains continued until the tenth century.

Despite being patrons of Sanatan Hinduism, the Satavahana kings exhibited remarkable tolerance towards other religions, evident in their support for Buddhist cave carvings. The initiation of cave carving at Ajanta during the Satavahana period is notable, with Caves No. 9 and No. 10 dating back to their rule. Inscriptions at Ajanta also attest that the renowned chaitya (shrine) at Karla and toranas (ornamental gateways) at the Sanchi stupa were created during this era. The chaitya at Karla, recognized as the world's largest, is celebrated for its intricate design. Additionally, the sculptures depicting the life of Buddha on the torana of the Sanchi stupa reflect the flourishing of art during the Satavahana period. This dynasty played a pivotal role in shaping the cultural and artistic landscape of south India, leaving an indelible mark on the region's history.

Out of around 1,200 carved caves in India, more than 1,000 of them are in Maharashtra alone. These caves are strategically located along ancient trade routes. The Satavahana dynasty's domestic and international trade was thriving. The caves were carved on the route that connected the north and south, and on the route that connected ports to commercial cities, to serve as varshavas for Buddhist monks who travelled across India to spread dhamma. The Satavahanas had robust international trade relations with Rome, Egypt, Italy and Greece. Exports from India were booming and Indian artefacts and ivory carvings, particularly from Maharashtra, were highly sought after in the global market. Evidence of these exports was discovered in the ancient city of Pompeii in Italy, buried under volcanic ash from Mount Vesuvius's eruption in 79 CE. Approximately 1,600 years later, excavations began with the discovery of Pompeii, which had been buried in volcanic ash. During the excavation, archaeologists found a small box containing an intricate sculpture of a woman carved out of ivory. The sculpture originated from Bhokardan in Maharashtra (where identical sculptures were found during excavations), a prominent trading centre during the Satavahana period. Carved ivory objects were made there and shipped elsewhere. The discovery suggested a trade connection dating back to the first century or perhaps even earlier.

The trade activities were not confined to Bhokardan alone; Ter (then Tagar) in Osmanabad district also played a significant role as a trading town during this period. The volume of trade is a testament to the skill of the Indian artisans of the time. The manuscript *Periplus of the Erythraean Sea*, written by a Greek merchant who visited India in the second century BCE, provides detailed insights into the trade relations between the Satavahanas and the Romans. Ports like Bhadoch, Sopara, Kalyan, Chaul, Jaigad, Dabhol, Rajapur and Bankot were vital hubs for this trade, with goods transported to Pratishthan through Tagar from three ports, namely Bhadoch, Sopara and Kalyan.

The economic prosperity from trade is evident in the five famous trading cities of Maharashtra during that time—Nashik, Junnar, Paithan, Ter and Bhokardan. Many remains of this prosperous trade have been found, and there is also a popular anecdote about the trade with Rome. During the Satavahana period, exports from India to Rome exceeded imports, resulting in a substantial influx of gold coins into India. Emperor Nero's reign from 54 CE to 68 CE saw a surge in imports from India, causing concerns about the Roman economy. There was much debate and discussion, which led to a proposal from the Roman cabinet to impose restrictions on trade with India. Pliny the Elder, the famous Roman encyclopaedist who held many positions of honour during Nero's reign, recorded this, shedding light on the prosperity of India during the Satavahana period. Further, during Emperor Nero's rule, his adversaries pressed him with a proposal to prohibit the import of pearls from India. In a rather amusing turn of events, Nero is said to have swayed these opponents by offering them pearls as bribes, successfully diverting any restrictions on large-scale pearl imports from India. The thriving trade undoubtedly contributed to Maharashtra's first-class economic status in India and the world during the Satavahana era. The wealth and prosperity derived from trade played a pivotal role in the flourishing of art, which is evident in the intricately carved caves and sculptures of the time.

King Hala Satavahana, known for his deep appreciation of literature, played an important role in the preservation and promotion of fine literary works during the Satavahana dynasty. One notable contribution is his editing of the text *Gaha Sattasai*, more commonly known by its Sanskrit name *Gathasaptashati*. This poetry anthology stands out for its collection of seven hundred gathas (verses) composed by the common people, particularly those from rural areas during that era. King Hala exhibited his commitment to literature by reportedly purchasing each gatha from the people at a lavish price during the compilation of this collection. Written in the Prakrit language, these gathas are considered the earliest examples of folk literature.

It is remarkable that *Gaha Sattasai*, a literary treasure that deviated from pre-existing religious traditions, originated in Maharashtra. Today, this Prakrit composition holds significance for a different reason: it played a crucial role in conferring the classical language status to Marathi, the official language of Maharashtra. To be recognized as a classical language by the government, one criterion is that the language should be 1,500 years old. Recognizing the potential of *Gaha Sattasai* to fulfil this criterion, experts used this text in the application for Marathi to be acknowledged as a classical language.

On the topic of language, it appears that the Satavahana kings were proponents of Prakrit. Stone inscriptions related to Satavahana kings discovered in Naneghat, Karla, Kanheri and Nashik are all in the Prakrit language. Notable inscriptions, such as Queen Naganika's at Naneghat and Balashree's in the Pandava cave at Nashik, describing Gautamiputra's bravery, have been invaluable for researchers and scholars in this field. Additionally, the famous writer Gunadhya is associated with the Satavahana kings, further emphasizing their patronage of literature and language during their rule.

The reign of the Satavahana dynasty, spanning from 235 BCE to 225 CE,[3] is regarded as a golden period for Maharashtra, lasting for around 450 years. This era witnessed the establishment of state power, the revival of religion, the promotion of arts, agricultural advancements, flourishing trade, and unprecedented wealth and prosperity. The Satavahanas significantly contributed to laying the cultural foundation of Maharashtra. Following the Satavahanas,

---

3 P.G. Sahastrabuddhe, *Maharashtra Sanskruti* (Continental Prakashan, 1979), p. 80.

the Vakatakas ascended to power in Maharashtra. It is speculated that their founder, Vindhyashakti, was a general of the Satavahana dynasty. The Vakatakas ruled for three centuries, from 250 CE to 550 CE. At the peak of their power, the Vakataka kingdom spread from north Bundelkhand to Hyderabad. While the Satavahanas contributed to the revival of the Vedic religion, the Vakatakas played a crucial role in safeguarding Hinduism and Hindu culture. In the 150 years following 225 CE, until the rise of the Gupta dynasty, no Hindu kings were as impactful and powerful as the Vakatakas. They, along with the Bharshiva dynasty of Vidisha, actively worked towards protecting Hindu dharma.

LEGACY OF THE VAKATAKA DYNASTY

Historian Kashiprasad Jayaswal attributes much of this credit to the Vakataka king Pravarasena-I. According to Jayaswal, King Pravarasena-I firmly propagated and implemented the idea that India should be ruled by Hindu emperors, with Hindu theology at the forefront. During the reign of Pravarasena-I's grandson Rudrasena, King Samudragupta of the north began establishing his empire, conquering most of north and south India. However, Rudrasena maintained the independence of the Vakataka kingdom, and there is no indication of a battle between Rudrasena and Samudragupta.

Rudrasena-II, son of Prithvisena, continued the legacy and formed an alliance with Emperor Chandragupta-II, assisting in the expulsion of Shaka Kshatrapas from Maval and Saurashtra. This alliance is believed to have contributed to the decline of Shaka Kshatrapas' power. Additionally, Rudrasena-II's marriage to Prabhavatigupta, Chandragupta-II's daughter, further solidified the friendly relations between the two kingdoms. Unfortunately,

Prabhavatigupta's marital harmony was short-lived as Rudrasena-II passed away within seven to eight years of their marriage. She exhibited great courage as a regent, supported by her father, until her minor sons Diwakarsena and Pravarasena-II reached maturity. This period reflects the political influence and strategic alliances that the Vakatakas wielded in the broader geopolitical landscape.

The Vakataka reign stands out as a flourishing period for both Sanskrit and Prakrit literature. This era witnessed the emergence of the Vaidarbhi style of Sanskrit poetry, a prominent literary form used by esteemed poets like Kalidasa. Kalidasa, who served as an officer and diplomat sent by Chandragupta to assist Prabhavati after the death of Rudrasena-II, composed his famous epic Meghdoot in the Vidarbha region of present-day Maharashtra during the Vakataka period. Notably, kings Sarvasena and Pravarsena-II of the Vakataka dynasty themselves were accomplished poets, contributing poetic texts titled *Harivijaya* and *Setubandha*, respectively. Interestingly, both works are composed in Maharashtrian Prakrit, and some of their Sanskrit epigrammatic poems (subhashitas) were included in later editions of *Gaha Sattasai*.

The Vakataka kings also served as patrons of the arts. Cave nos. 16, 17 and 19 at Ajanta, carved during the Vakataka period, are celebrated for their unique architecture, sculptures and paintings and have garnered praise from art scholars. Additionally, the Vakatakas contributed to the development of temple architecture, popularizing the construction of temples near villages in the fourth century CE. The Trivikrama Temple at Ter (then Tagarpur) in Osmanabad district is considered the oldest temple in Maharashtra, made of floating bricks and dating back to the distinctive Vakataka period. It remains in good condition today, along with other ancient temples in the same village constructed using floating bricks.

Pravarasena's notable contributions include the construction of the Pravareshwar Temple and the Shri Ramchandra Temple at Ramtek. Numerous temples and cave sculptures from this period have been discovered, suggesting a vibrant cultural and historical landscape during the Vakataka reign and a sense of security from foreign invasion in Maharashtra at that time.

CHALUKYAS AND THE RISE OF THE RASHTRAKUTAS

After the Vakatakas, the Chalukyas of Badami assumed control in Maharashtra. From 550 CE to 753 CE, for 300 years, the Chalukyas ruled over the region extending from Narmada to Rameshwar in the south. Among them, Satyasraya Pulakeshi-II, the grandson of Satyasraya Pulakeshi, emerged as the most powerful king and expanded the kingdom from north to south, earning the title of 'Trisamudratapitavahana', like the Satavahana king Gautamiputra Satakarni.

In 736 CE, when present-day Gujarat was under Chalukya control, Arabs attempted to take control of the region. Despite the Arabs having already conquered Konkan, Kutch and Saurashtra, the Chalukya warrior King Pulakeshi thwarted their efforts. Additionally, the Chalukyas prevented northern kings, who were seeking territorial expansion, from making inroads into the south.

Some scholars say that the Chalukyas are known more for their cultural activities than their political achievements. This statement is a testimony to the Chalukya contribution to the development of various art forms. Murals at Ajanta and the Vaishnava and Jain temples at Badami, dating back to the Chalukya period, exemplify advancements in the art of carving. The architectural strides during the Chalukya period were so remarkable that a new style of sculpture created at that time is now known as the Chalukya style of architecture. The sculptures at Malagatti in Badami, Meguti in Aihole, and Sangameshwara, Papanatha, and Virupaksha temples at Pattadakal showcase unparalleled beauty, affirming the Chalukyas' role in pushing the development of arts to new heights.

In this artistically opulent land, the Rashtrakuta dynasty came to power after the Chalukyas. Initially serving as samants (feudatories) of the Chalukyas, the Rashtrakutas later established their own rule. King Krishnaraj of the Rashtrakuta clan notably constructed the Kailasa Temple at Ellora in the eighth century. By then, the tradition of carving caves in Maharashtra had gone on for a thousand years, reaching its zenith. As previously discussed, there was unparalleled development in the art of sculpture in the southern regions during the Chalukya rule. Further, the Rashtrakutas maintained amicable relations with the Pallava kings of the south, who were known for constructing temples rich in architecture and sculptures. Intermarriages between members of these two clans further attest to their friendly ties—thus, the Pallavas had influence over the Rashtrakutas. The unique design of the sculpture-rich Kailasa cave temple resulted from the amalgamation of the Chalukya style and Pallava art. The influence of the Chalukya style on this temple is detailed in the previous chapter, along with evidence supporting the attribution of its construction to King Krishnaraj. Undeniably unique, the Kailasa Temple captivates observers with its carved, beautiful sculptural features set against the backdrop of the mountain into which it is intricately carved. Examining the broader history of architecture, sculptures and paintings in Maharashtra, it becomes evident that our predecessors deserve credit for the creation of the awe-inspiring Kailasa Temple.

3

A KING'S GRAND DREAM: THE BRIHADEESWARA TEMPLE

The sculptures of Dwarapalas (guardians of the temple) and depictions of Shiva on the southern wall of the Brihadeeswara Temple at Thanjavur, Tamil Nadu

A panaromic view of the breathtaking Brihadeeshwara Temple complex at Thanjavur, Tamil Nadu

A granite sculpture of a Dwarapala (guardian) at Brihadeeswara Temple in Thanjavur, Tamil Nadu

Inscriptions on the gopura wall at Brihadeeswara Temple in Tamil Nadu that provides information about the temple dancers, highlighting that dance was considered a form of worship

India boasts a rich and venerable history, having been the homeland of numerous powerful royal dynasties that not only ensured stable governance but also ushered prosperity into their realms. The various art forms that developed during the period are a testament to this, evident from the sculptures, architecture, paintings and statues from that period that are preserved even today. The wonderful confluence of these can be seen in many ancient temples of south India.

Among these, the Chola dynasty's monarchs stand out as great patrons of the arts. They elevated various art forms to their zenith through the construction of exquisite temples, with these temple complexes representing the pinnacle of Chola architects' achievements.

My long-held fascination with these temples culminated in a vacation in December 2019, leading me and my husband, Vinod, to explore Trichy, Thanjavur and Kumbakonam in Tamil Nadu. The abundance of ancient temples in the region posed a challenge—deciding which ones to exclude rather than which to visit during our trip. However, the foremost temples of the Chola empire, namely the Brihadeeswara Temple in Thanjavur, the Shiva Temple in Gangaikonda Cholapuram and the Airavatesvara Temple in Darasuram, were at the top of our must-see list.

Despite the centuries that have passed since their construction, these three magnificent temples, collectively known as the 'Great Living Chola Temples', stand in impeccable condition. Recognized as UNESCO World Heritage sites, they are a testament to the enduring legacy of Chola architecture. The Brihadeeswara Temple in Thanjavur, in particular, earned the prestigious designation in 1987.

After flying from Mumbai to Trichy, we dedicated the first day to exploring the important temples in the region. We arrived at Thanjavur by night, to visit the next stop—the Brihadeeswara Temple, also known as the 'Dakshina Meru' (Mount Meru of the south). In order to explore the temple with a fresh mind and with ample time to ourselves, we planned an early visit at 7.30 a.m. the next morning.

Rising at 5 a.m., we were greeted by the sounds of early-morning traffic, signalling the bustling start to the day in Thanjavur. After getting dressed, we enjoyed a hearty breakfast of warm, soft idlis and delicious sambar. The morning air felt crisp and pleasant as we set out for the temple. Our hotel was conveniently located nearby but given the town's popularity among tourists and the ongoing winter holidays, we opted to leave early.

As we travelled, we immersed ourselves in the quintessential sights and scents of a quaint small town. Tiny temples blared devotional music through loudspeakers, locals flocked to idli-vada stalls for a quick breakfast, and the enchanting fragrance of jasmine emanated from large woven baskets filled with garlands made of fresh flowers, skilfully sold by beautiful women dressed in sarees.

Upon our arrival, the spacious parking lot opposite the temple was nearly at capacity. Vendors had set up shop on the footpath adjacent to the temple, showcasing traditional Thanjavur dancing dolls—a unique toy that is a speciality of Thanjavur. These intricately crafted, bobble-headed terracotta dolls create a mesmerizing dance illusion through their deliberate, oscillatory movements. While parents hurried towards the temple, their children were drawn to the captivating dolls.

Observing the congested parking lot, bustling footpath and crowded streets, I briefly pondered over whether we would be able to fully appreciate the temple amidst the influx of people. However, as we stepped out of the car, a breathtaking view unfolded before us—fortified stone walls, three majestic gopuras, and the temple standing proudly behind them. The sight was so captivating that I found it difficult to divert my gaze. I recalled the words of an expert who had marvelled at these grand gopuras adorned with intricate sculptures, deeming them 'the most impressive, the largest, and most ambitious creation in temple architecture'.

Motivated by these words, I had begun learning more about King Rajaraja Chola, the visionary behind the temple's construction. The more I discovered about his valour, passion for art and literature, and administrative prowess, the more engrossed I became in the rich history surrounding this architectural masterpiece.

THE RISE OF THE CHOLAS

To fully appreciate the history of the Brihadeeswara Temple, delving into the legacy of its creator, King Rajaraja Chola, becomes paramount. To begin, one has to look at the history of the Chola dynasty. This dynasty was a powerhouse that wielded immense influence in southern India from ancient times.

The Chola dynasty stood as one of the most powerful and long-ruling dynasties in south India. Identifying themselves as Suryavanshi (descendants of Surya, the Hindu sun god) and descendants of the renowned theologian Manu, the Cholas left their indelible mark, even earning mentions in the Mahabharata. The earliest references to the Cholas are found in ancient texts and inscriptions, which trace their lineage to the Sangam period, specifically the second to third century CE. It is widely believed, although not entirely clear, that they were extremely influential in the second century but that over the years, their importance waned and they became vassals—subjugated rulers pledging allegiance in the form of taxes and military support—to powers such as the Pallavas, Chalukyas and Rashtrakutas.

The reason for the lack of clarity is that there is insufficient knowledge about the history of south India from the third to ninth century CE. Yet, records of enmity between the Pallavas and the Cholas are available. The celebrated Chinese traveller, Hiuen Tsang, who documented his visit to India from 630 CE to 644 CE, mentions the Cholas in his writings.

The eighth and ninth centuries witnessed the decline of the Pallavas and the Pandyas, setting the stage for the Chola dynasty's resurgence. Capitalizing on the rivalry between the Pandyas and the Pallavas, King Vijayalaya Chola (who reigned from 850 CE to 871 CE), a shrewd vassal of the Pallavas, conquered Thanjavur and established it as the new capital. The credit for restoring the lost glory of the Chola dynasty is attributed to him. His successors, King Aditya-I and King Parantaka-I, followed, although the history of the Chola dynasty for the subsequent thirty-two years remains relatively obscure.

King Rajaraja, born in 947 CE, ascended the throne at the mature age of thirty-eight in 985 CE. The reason for his delayed succession is explained later in this chapter. Recognized as a formidable monarch and a brilliant strategist, he swiftly solidified his kingdom's standing by decisively dealing with the Chola enemies, reinstating Chola power and establishing their supremacy in south India.

His strategic manoeuvres commenced with the subjugation of the Cheras and the Pandyas from Kerala, whose recurrent attacks had troubled the Chola empire. A crowning achievement was the establishment of a robust naval fleet, enabling him to expand his kingdom southward by conquering the Maldives islands. Another high point of his naval campaigns was the successful invasion of Ceylon, consolidating his rule over the region and expanding the Chola empire. He also valiantly attempted to defeat the powerful Rashtrakutas. During his reign, this mighty ruler brought the entire southern part of India up to the Tungabhadra river under his control.

While King Rajaraja established his supremacy and extended his kingdom through numerous military conquests, he did not focus solely on the expansion of his territory. This warrior king has also been recorded in history as an able administrator due to the leviathan land assessment survey he undertook and the local self-governments he established. He was also known to be a strong advocate for the expansion of trade. Recognizing the significance of revenue from trade, King Rajaraja strategically sought to control the maritime trade route connecting Southeast Asia. Through well-organized military campaigns, he ensured the stability and control of this crucial trade route. By fostering trade and diplomatic ties with foreign kings, he brought both stability and prosperity to his kingdom.

Political stability faced dual threats from foreign invasions and internal uprisings. King Rajaraja adeptly addressed both challenges. To secure future stability, he imparted comprehensive lessons and practical governance experience to his son, Rajendra. This deliberate preparation not only eliminated disputes over inheritance but also further stabilized the Chola empire. King Rajaraja ruled his kingdom for twenty-nine years until his death in 1014 CE, cementing his name in the annals of history as a just and gallant ruler.

King Rajaraja's reign and those of his successors marked a golden era for learning and the arts in the Chola dynasty. Advancements in architecture and sculpture flourished, and the distinctive

Dravidian influence became prominent during this period. The Cholas, especially under King Rajaraja, made remarkable strides in architecture, with the Brihadeeswara Temple standing as a testament to their artistic and engineering prowess.

BEFORE ENTERING THE BRIHADEESWARA TEMPLE

Constructed between 1004 CE and 1010 CE, the Brihadeeswara Temple is an architectural masterpiece, showcasing the pinnacle of Dravidian architecture. Spanning an impressive 240.79 metres from east to west and 121.92 metres from north to south, the temple adheres strictly to the axial and symmetrical rules of geometry. What makes this achievement even more remarkable is that the entire project was completed in just six years without access to modern-day technology. A distinctive feature of this temple is that it is made entirely of granite; the construction required 1,30,000 tonnes of granite. It is considered to be a model of pure architecture—i.e., the entire structure from the lowest step to the pinnacle is crafted using a single building material, granite in this case. Since granite was not available in the vicinity, it had to be transported from a distance of about 30–40 kilometres away from the temple site. In fact, in 2010, commemorating the temple's 1,000[th] anniversary, the Government of India issued a coin with a denomination of rupees 1,000, made from 80 per cent silver and 20 per cent copper.

We now stood before this magnificent structure. Before entering, one can see the fortified walls surrounding it. The strong ramparts have a moat around them and are reminiscent of those seen protecting ancient citadels. After the original ramparts collapsed, they were rebuilt by the Nayakas during the sixteenth century. Upon entering the temple premises, we first came across a stone gateway called the 'Maratha Gate', deriving its name from the period of over 150 years when the Marathas ruled over Thanjavur. Their rule began in 1674 CE when King Vyankoji Bhosale, the step-brother of Chhatrapati Shivaji Maharaj, defeated Alagiri Nayak and secured the throne. The Marathas ruled Thanjavur for a long time until the formal annexation of the kingdom by the British in 1855 CE. During that period, they built the 'Maratha Gate', the first entrance to the Brihadeeswara Temple among their many substantial works.

After crossing the Maratha Gate, one faces the Keralantakan Tiruvasala gopura, which was constructed by King Rajaraja to commemorate his victory over the Cheras of Kerala, and following that is the Rajarajan Tiruvasala gopura. On the façade of Rajarajan Tiruvasala gopura, one is met with the stunning carvings of dwarapalas (guardians of the entrance to a temple), which is a common feature in many Chola temples. The tall monolithic granite columns are a wonder to behold! It makes one wonder how such huge slabs of granite were carried to this site. The columns of the gopuras are also carved from granite, and the upper portions are made of bricks. The columns are adorned with carvings of beautiful idols. In fact, it gives one a preview of the fine sculptures to be seen within the temple. Mythological stories about Lord Shiva's life are carved on the Rajarajan Tiruvasala gopura. The sculptures of Lord Shiva and Goddess Parvati dancing captivate the viewer. The sculptures are a depiction of a mythological story in which the two had a row over who was the superior dancer and eventually held a competition, with Lord Vishnu as the judge. This sculpture highlights the importance of dance as an art form during this period. King Rajaraja had given generous patronage to artists who had mastered Bharatanatyam—the classical dance form of Tamil Nadu, by giving them a prestigious platform to showcase their dancing skills, making the temple a refuge for dancers. The temple depicts eighty-one postures of Bharatanatyam, suggesting the significance of this classical dance form by the early eleventh century. Further, the 108 types of Shiva's Tandava dance (divine dance) are carved on the upper level of the garbhagriha (the sanctum sanctorum). During that period, nearly 400 dancers and 250 musicians were in residence at the temple. Since playing a musical instrument and singing were considered to be the fourteenth recognized form, and dance as the fifteenth recognized form of the worship of God, prayers in the form of dancing and singing were offered to God every morning, afternoon and evening. The Tamil inscriptions carved on the gopuras shed light on this as well as provide details of the dancers assigned to the temple, their names and their respective proficiency in acting, postures, agility, their salary and awards bestowed upon them by the king in the form of money or land.

After having looked at the gopuras, we were treated to a view of the clean and sprawling temple premises. My fear of not being able to see the temple properly, given the number of tourist buses in the parking lot, was unfounded, as the vast temple premises could easily accommodate all. We were simply mesmerized by the lofty structures before us—the multi-pillared Nandi mandapa in front of us and on the right side an open courtyard for yajnas. Further right, abutting the entirety of the outer wall of the temple, on both sides, are narrow structures. During the reign of King Rajaraja and his successors, the structures would be overrun by dancers and musicians excitedly preparing themselves for a performance since the area served as the resident quarters of the artists.

While taking in all of these marvellous sights, our attention was drawn to the glossy black sculpture of Nandi, the vahana (vehicle) of Lord Shiva, used by him as a means of transport, and our feet automatically veered towards it. A crowd of tourists had formed around the Nandi sculpture, which is located in the centre of the Nandi mandapa. Reaching closer, we realized that the tourists were thronging the area, desperate to click a picture with the mammoth Nandi. It rests on a tall, compact plinth and is carved out of a monolithic block of granite with a height of 13 feet and length of 16 feet.[4] Approximately 100 metres away from the main Shivalinga, with its proportionate folded legs, chains adorned with beads and bells around its neck, large eyes and stubby horns, the Nandi is a remarkable sight! While entranced by the beauty of the sculpture, the beautifully painted ceiling of the Nandi mandapa caught my eye. With its artistic paintings that use an array of colour combinations, the ceiling is a testament to the glory of the art of this period. The beautifully painted ceiling is credited to the Nayakas, who decorated the ceiling during their reign in the sixteenth century. I thought to myself that these priceless treasures need to be preserved for future generations. As this thought crossed my mind, I remembered that various rituals, investitures and consecrations are performed regularly in this World Heritage Site status-accorded temple, including on the Nandi. The Nandi is bathed regularly with aromatic essences and sometimes draped with a vastra (cloth). At such times, the tourists coming from all over the world, unable to see the beautiful Nandi, are likely to be disheartened. We were disheartened as well, since when we visited, the Nandi's head was covered with a white cloth. Nevertheless, we clicked a picture beside the Nandi to commemorate our visit.

The warm sunshine had chased away the chilly weather of early morning now. As we turned away from the Nandi mandapa, we

---

4 www.tamilnadutourism.tn.gov.in/destinations/brihadeeswara-temple

beheld the majestic main temple before us, so vast that it could not be contained in our field of vision. A few steps away from the Nandi mandapa is a verandah with a stone roof supported by multiple pillars. The roof above the steps ends with a specially carved semicircular form. This may have been specifically carved to drain out rainwater from the sides and prevent it from collecting on the roof. Amusingly, a lizard climbing the ceiling has also been carved on its surface. Beyond the verandah is an enclosed rectangular building consisting of an ardha mandapa (half-open hall) and a maha mandapa (great gathering hall). There are a few windows on this wall with beautifully carved stone mesh frames. Beyond this, the garbhagriha and a towering superstructure can be seen. In south Indian temple architecture, the sanctum sanctorum and the tower above it are collectively called the vimana. The external surface of the tower is carved to mimic Mount Kailasa, the abode of Lord Shiva, and is decorated with several sculptures of deities such as Shiva and his sons, Kartikeya and Ganesha. The vimana is sixty-six metres tall, upon which rests a spherical summit termed the kumbhak with a circumference of 7.8 metres, weighing a whopping eighty tonnes. Local guides and several authorities say that the kumbhak is made up of a single block of stone. However, this information is incorrect. Renowned historian R.K. Nagaswamy, who is the erstwhile head of the Tamil Nadu Department of Archaeology, and has been the recipient of the prestigious Padma Bhushan award for his valuable contribution in this field, has disproved this theory. According to him, the kumbhak is made up of several stones, which are joined together.

This temple has been built employing not only architectural but also engineering prowess, which is evident from the various unique features of the temple. One of these is that, from the entrance to the sanctum sanctorum, the temple is built in an exact straight line, which stretches from the east to the west. This temple was exceptionally architecturally advanced compared to other contemporary south Indian temples of the time. In south Indian temples, it was typical for the entrance or gopuras to be higher than the main temple. However, the main temple of the Brihadeeswara complex was at a record-breaking height in the tenth century and although the gopuras are towering, they are not as tall as the main temple. Another surprising fact is that this temple, which stands tall at a height of sixty-six metres, has not tilted even slightly in the thousand years since its construction. This is truly an astonishing feature and living proof of the advanced engineering skills of India at the time! It is even more impressive when one considers that its foundation is said to be only five feet deep. Slight tilting has occurred in most of the structures built around the same time or a little later, in even those of a lesser height. An example is the Leaning Tower of Pisa in Italy, whose construction started in 1173 CE and was finally completed in 1372 CE, although the delay is attributable to various difficulties in building. Despite it having taken 200 years to be built, its height of fifty-seven metres pales in comparison to the Brihadeehwara Temple, which was built in a mere six years. Soon after the construction of the tower in Pisa, it started leaning, and in spite of the myriad measures taken to prevent it from leaning, it has tilted by four degrees. This history is seen to have been repeated in various other buildings all over the world, which is why the Brihadeeswara Temple, which has firmly withstood natural calamities such as earthquakes and storms for over a thousand years!

It is said that the shadow of this temple never falls on the ground, but this premise is entirely incorrect. There is an amusing anecdote that may have given rise to this conjecture which, of course, is uncorroborated by any historical evidence. The story goes that when the temple was completed, King Rajaraja was inspecting it while accompanied by the chief architect. King Rajaraja was impressed since it was exactly how he had envisioned it. However, looking at the stupendous temple, he was struck by an intrusive thought. 'Will this temple ever fall in the future?' he mused. The architect jokingly retorted, 'Forget the temple, its shadow also can never fall on the ground.'

KING RAJARAJA'S GRAND VISION

As I stood staring at the temple, looking at the exquisite carvings on the vimana, I began a guessing game trying to identify the deities portrayed in the sculptures. I then focused on their style—whether they were upright or seated, the ornaments, the weapons and equipment they were holding. Suddenly, I felt a crick in my neck and realized that I had been looking up at the vimana for a long time. Despite this, I was yet to see all the deities right up to the summit of the vimana. Looking at this commendable undertaking instilled awe and a sense of pride within me. King Rajaraja dreamt of this grand temple and brought it to fruition within six years. It must have been a source of employment for many engineers, architects, sculptors, and artists, who must have received so much inspiration and encouragement. Once completed, the temple was a centre for music, dance, culture, trade and social and political affairs. In that period, the Brihadeeswara Temple must have served as a forum for all the meritorious people in the state to meet and interact.

    I wondered what inspired King Rajaraja to build this magnificent temple. What could have been the motivating force behind it? King

Rajaraja was a devotee of Lord Shiva, and it is said that he built this temple to honour Lord Shiva so that the lord's blessing would always be bestowed on his kingdom. Another theory is that he may have been inspired by the temples built by the Pallavas. While searching for the true cause that inspired King Rajaraja, I came across a remarkably interesting dramatized theory propounded in an episode of *Bharat Ek Khoj*, an Indian historical drama.

As stated earlier, King Rajaraja ascended the throne in 985 CE at the age of thirty-eight. This was a period marked by suspicion and distrust between the members of the Chola dynasty. King Sundara Chola (also known as Parantaka-II), Rajaraja's father, was to be succeeded to the Chola throne by his eldest son. However, when King Sundara Chola was at an advanced age and terribly ill, his eldest son died young, in a purported accident. It is theorized that this accident was, in fact, a murder plotted by his uncle Uttama Chola, borne out of greed for the throne. This theory is strengthened by Uttama Chola's immediate declaration of himself as the king, saying that Rajaraja was too young to rule. Despite King Sundara Chola's wish that Rajaraja should ascend the throne once he was of age, Uttama Chola did not hand over the throne to Rajaraja when he attained adulthood and instead gave him duties as his deputy. Rajaraja held this post for sixteen years, until the death of his uncle, after which he ascended the throne. Uttama Chola's death was an unnatural one and considered to be due to poisoning. This created a situation of distrust. According to some, Uttama was killed by the Chalukyas but many people cast aspersions upon Rajaraja, blaming him for the murder of his uncle for the throne. Unfortunately, even his own grandmother believed this to be true, which led to a falling out between them. Saddened by his revered grandmother's lack of trust in him, Rajaraja tried to convince her of his innocence several times, without any success. Finally, in desperation, he asked her how he could remedy the situation. She relented at last and told him to build a temple in memory of his uncle. In spite of the bitter feelings Rajaraja held towards his uncle due to the treacherous cold-blooded murder of his elder brother, he agreed to build the temple out of his abounding love and respect for his grandmother.

During the intervening period, Rajaraja strengthened the administration of his kingdom, deploying the skills he had developed in his time as deputy. Having realized the importance of trade, he improved trade and political relations with kingdoms in Southeast Asia including the kingdom of Cambodia. While thinking of the temple to be built in his uncle's memory, Rajaraja encountered a group of merchants who had returned from Cambodia after a profitable trip. The merchants had met him to complain about being unfairly robbed of their earnings by the navy of the Cheras of Kerala. The merchants then gave King Rajaraja a special gift given by the King of Cambodia—a golden miniature replica of a Hindu temple built in Cambodia. The merchants sang praises of the massive and stunning temple they had seen in Cambodia. Some of the merchants even expressed their desire to see such a temple in the Chola kingdom. However, since King Rajaraja was preoccupied with armed threats from the Cheras and other military campaigns for consolidating his empire, the matter did not go any further.

Eventually, King Rajaraja's grandmother selected a suitable site to construct the temple and hired an architect of her choice, who submitted a blueprint for the temple. The grandmother-approved blueprint seemed extremely ordinary to King Rajaraja, due to which he did not approve the design. His grandmother, however, felt that King Rajaraja deliberately disapproved of the plan as a dilatory tactic.

King Rajaraja had a grand vision for the temple; he wanted to build something monumental, an idea that may have taken root from the golden replica of the temple in Cambodia. Accordingly, he began searching for the right person who could make his dream come true. He discussed his vision at length with his mentor and advisor Guru Karuvurar Devar and sought recommendations for an able and skilled architect. A master of all trades, Guru Karuvurar Devar had expertise in architecture. He suggested that the architect Kunjara Mallan Raja Rama Perunthachan would do justice to this project. King Rajaraja then invited the architect and narrated his dream. An open-minded architect, Kunjara Mallan welcomed the king's fresh ideas with enthusiasm and prepared a blueprint capturing the king's vision perfectly. Extremely pleased and impressed by the plan, King Rajaraja confirmed Kunjara Mallan's appointment for the construction of the temple.

However, these developments did not go down well with King Rajaraja's grandmother, who vehemently opposed the plan and accused the king of deliberately delaying the construction. The tensions between the two increased by the day, and there were constant arguments. By now, the plans of the temple the king had commissioned were taking definite shape, and he was keen to execute the plan according to his ideas. Realizing that he would not be able to see eye-to-eye with his grandmother on the sensitive subject of the temple in the name of his uncle, he entrusted the supervision of the construction of his uncle's temple to his grandmother so that he could concentrate on his dream project, which would be built in his own name.

Thus, the embodiment of King Rajaraja's dream and vision is before us in the form of Brihadeeswara Temple. His mentor,

Guru Karuvurar Devar and architect Kunjara Mallan Raja Rama Perunthachan too have played an integral role in its creation. It is said that King Rajaraja was able to achieve greatness in large part due to his guru's guidance in various fields of governance. A painting depicting King Rajaraja with his guru is displayed in an inner part of the temple, although we did not get a chance to see it. There is also a small temple within the premises that is dedicated to the guru. It should be noted, however, that while there are numerous references to Guru Karuvurar Devar being King Rajaraja's mentor, some historians do not accept it because of a lack of evidence. King Rajaraja thus showcased his strength and power to the world, through the medium of this temple, which is why it has always been known as Rajarajeshwaram from its inception. Certain sources state that the temple came to be known as the Brihadeeswara Temple during the reign of the Marathas.

INSIDE THE BRIHADEESWARA TEMPLE

As we approached the temple, its entire history flashed through my mind. With the sun having risen fully, it had now become much warmer. Tourists who had finished seeing the temple were seeking shelter under its shade and chatting animatedly. Young girls dressed in traditional south Indian bordered skirts were wandering around the premises and children were running about like the wind in the open areas of the temple complex. Some tourists were sparing no effort in trying to achieve the impossible task of capturing the entire temple from top to bottom within their camera frame. They pulled out all the stops—trying different angles with their cameras, bending over backwards, and even trying sitting and sleeping positions to achieve the desired effect. It struck my mind that even the sophisticated cameras of today are unable to capture the entirety of King Rajaraja's massive creation.

We took the steps to the main entrance of the temple, having decided to first take a look at the interior of the temple and then see the beautiful sculptures carved on the outer walls. Upon entering the main entrance, one encounters fine carvings of male figures on the walls adjoining it. These are carvings of the mighty kings of the Chola dynasty. We climbed the stairs and saw that even in the verandah-like area, the ceiling had beautiful carvings. As we headed towards the sanctum sanctorum, people moved along in single file for darshan, first crossing the ardha mandapa then the maha mandapa. Even though the huge Shivalinga was visible from afar, when we stood right before it, we were transfixed by the sight. The linga is 8.7 metres in height with a circumference of 16.7 metres. After seeing it, I realized why it was referred to as Brihad Eeshwara (literally meaning massive god, a reference to Lord Shiva). The interior of the vimana is thirteen storeys tall and hollow, while the exterior is adorned with sculptures. Since Brihad Eeshwara is worshipped here daily, a raised platform has been constructed for the temple's priests to perform various rituals. We were already very impressed with the grandeur of the architecture of the temple right from the first gopura to the sanctum sanctorum, but the vision of the majestic Brihad Eeshwara was overwhelming. At a loss for words, we bowed down before it. During the time we had visited, preparations were in full swing for the great Mahakumbham festival to be held in February, due to which repairs and renovations were being undertaken. We were slightly disappointed that we were unable to see the temple entirely.

As we stepped outside after offering our prayers to the linga, the carvings on the outer walls caught our attention. The lower level of the vimana is called bhumi (land/earth), and it is thirteen metres tall; on its outer southern, western and northern walls, one can see engraved sculptures of deities. Most of the sculptures are housed inside artistically decorated frames. One is mesmerized by the beautifully carved idols of Vishnu, Shiva, Durga, Ganesh, Shridevi, Bhudevi and Lakshmi. The different forms of Lord Shiva are also depicted on these walls—Bhikshatana, Virbhadra, Kalantaka, Nataraja, Harihara, Chandrashekhara, Ardhanarishwar, Gangadhara, Alingana Chandrashekhara, Bhairava, Dakshinamurti, Sadashiva and many more. A typical feature of Chola temples is the lingodbhava, a magnificent idol of Lord Shiva emerging from the linga, usually located on the western side of the temple. This feature is seen here too. On either side of the lingodbhava are the idols of Brahma and Vishnu bowing before Shiva.

The temple has some characteristic bas-relief sculptures representing the five avasthitha (forms inspired by elements which make the Universe) of Lord Shiva. They are the Sadyojaat–Prithvitattva (inspired by earth, a symbol of kriya shakti or driving force), Tatpurush–Vayutattva (inspired by air, a symbol of pran shakti or life force), Aghor–Agnitattva (inspired by fire, a symbol of ichha shakti or willpower), Vaamdeva–Jalatattva (inspired by water, a symbol of dnyana shakti or the power of knowledge) and Ishaan–Akaashtattva (inspired by the sky, a symbol of atindriya shakti or transcendental power). Avasthitha sculptures are an extremely rare occurrence in temples. Other interesting sculptures include—Shata Rudra, the first 100 rays of the sun, which remained on earth in human form, and deities of the eight directions (Indra, Agni, Yama, Nirutti, Ishaan, Varun, Kuber, Vayu) are also seen on the vimana. As King Rajaraja was a great devotee of Shiva, he was given the title of Shivapadasevaka, which roughly translates to 'the worshipper of Lord Shiva'. Despite being a devout disciple of Lord Shiva, one finds numerous sculptures of Lord Vishnu and his incarnations in the temple. There is evidence that King Rajaraja was accepting of all faiths and religions. One such instance is that he had given permission and financial support to Shri Vijayattunga Varman of the Shailendra dynasty, the ruler of Srivijaya (modern-day Indonesia), to build the Chudamani Buddhist monastery in King Rajaraja's kingdom at Nagapattinam.

One of the unique features of this temple is the inscription carved on the adhishtan (lowermost portion) of the outer walls of the southern, western and northern sides of the entire temple. Similar inscriptions can also be seen on the gopuras. They describe the importance of Lord Brihadeeswara and give information about the festivals and ceremonies held in the temple. They also speak of the greatness of the sixteen Chola predecessors of King Rajaraja. These inscriptions give details about the construction of the temple, the donations received for its construction and accounts of the deposits and expenditure, reflecting King Rajaraja's meticulous planning. It also shows that King Rajaraja considered himself accountable to his subjects. Such minute planning and its rigorous implementation are seldom seen in history. King Rajaraja did not take sole credit for the construction of the temple and expressed his gratitude to the thousands of people involved in the project—from the cook to the chief architect—by engraving their names on the walls of the temple. After the construction of the temple, King Rajaraja made a conscious effort to make it known that the temple did not belong solely to him or a particular town but to all citizens. The neighbouring towns were given the responsibility of guarding the temple, with each town being assigned a specified day on which people were given a daily allowance and conveyance fees for this duty. This fostered a sense of responsibility and community among the people.

The events of that period are well preserved in the form of these inscriptions, giving us an opportunity to delve into the history of that period. King Rajaraja is also responsible for the preservation of another important literary work. In the period from the sixth to the tenth centuries, there were sixty-three Shaivite saints (followers of Lord Shiva) or Nayanars. These Nayanars composed devotional hymns in praise of Lord Shiva. By the time of King Rajaraja's reign in the tenth century, these compositions were almost forgotten. One day, a group of pilgrims came to the king's court and recited a hymn composed by a Nayanar. The devout King Rajaraja was taken with the beautiful composition. He felt that such excellent works must be preserved for posterity. However, since no one knew whether or where they existed, it was an almost impossible task. Guru Karuvurar Devar suggested that Nambiyandar Nambi would be able to assist them in this task. The king performed some religious rites as suggested by Nambi, after which Nambi had a divine realization that these compositions were preserved in the Thillai Nataraja Temple. While many efforts to obtain the literature were made, the orthodox priests of the Thillai Nataraja Temple refused to part with it. Finally, through King Rajaraja's intervention, the manuscripts were obtained. The manuscripts were in a dilapidated state, with some pages disintegrating while others were infested with termites. Despite these challenges, they were copied accurately and the compilation of the devotional compositions of the sixty-three Nayanars was named Tirumura. King Rajaraja helped save them from the brink of oblivion. These works show the expansion and development of the philosophy of the Shaivite sect for a period spanning 600 years. Tirumarai was a critical contribution to literary history that was made possible by King Rajaraja, preserving these ancient religious texts for future generations. In honour of this achievement, King Rajaraja was conferred the title of Tirumuraikanda Chola (the Chola who saved the Tirumurai). It is said that to create awareness about these beautiful hymns and to ensure that they did not fade into obscurity, the king employed fifty singers to sing these devotional compositions in the temple.

As we proceeded to view the sculptures on the façade, we noticed two smaller temples at the rear end, which were facing south. One temple, engraved with excellent carvings, is dedicated to Lord Kartikeya and was built by the Nayakas in the sixteenth century. The other one is dedicated to Lord Ganesha and is said to be built by the Marathas in the eighteenth century. These temples do not in any way diminish the beauty of the main temple. Unfortunately, we were unable to view the interior of these temples as they were under repair at the time. Besides these, there are other exquisitely carved temples dedicated to Parvati, Nataraja and the Nayanar Chandeshwar. We now headed towards a corridor-like area in the north of the premises. This area is attached to the outer wall of the temple and is said to have been built by King Rajaraja's army chief. It was allegedly built on the premise that just as the army chief protects the king, this area adjoining the outer wall protects the temple built by the king. This corridor is lined with a row of Shivalingas. The wall behind bears beautiful murals that were commissioned by the Nayakas. The main temple also houses invaluable paintings of the Chola era on the second and third floors, which were made using natural dyes. However, this area is closed to the public for the conservation of the paintings.

We had now circumambulated the temple and reached the Nandi mandapa once again. There is so much to see at this temple that despite having finished exploring the entire temple complex, the fear of having missed something beset me. We sat on the benches on the lawn and looked at the entire temple one last time. Looking at this magnificent, vast structure with its rich heritage of art and architecture, I could not help but think that the Brihadeeswara Temple and the valiant King Rajaraja Chola were immortalized here, and they will never fade from my memory.

4

THE ICONIC BRIHADEESWARA TEMPLE AT GANGAIKONDACHOLAPURAM

After seeing the oldest temple of the 'Great Living Chola Temples', the Brihadeeswara Temple at Thanjavur, we headed to our next destination, the Shiva temple at Gangaikondacholapuram. Gangaikondacholapuram is about seventy-two kilometres from Thanjavur. Soon after leaving the city, the scenery started to change rapidly. From our car, we observed stunning vast expanses of lush green paddy fields as far as the eye could see, and flocks of birds soaring in the clear blue sky. During the journey, we would occasionally stumble upon a tiny village. We would see small mud huts and brick houses, kids running around and the hustle and bustle of daily life in the village. These scenes, which for us captured the very essence of life, were heartwarming. As we neared our destination, the curiosity in my mind about the Gangaikondacholapuram Temple increased.

Like the Shiva temple in Thanjavur, this temple is also known by the name 'Brihadeeswar'. This temple is said to be a replica of the exquisitely beautiful Brihadeeswar Temple of Thanjavur. It was built by the mighty King Rajendra Chola-I, the son of King Rajaraja who had built the temple at Thanjavur. This temple, built in 1035 CE, is considered a prime example of Dravidian architecture. However, before that, the place where the temple is situated, Gangaikondacholapuram, was established as a new capital city by Rajendra Chola-I between 1023 CE to 1027 CE.[5] The story behind why Gangaikondacholapuram was established and given the status of capital, when the wealthy and prosperous Thanjavur already served as the capital of the Chola kingdom, is found within the name 'Gangaikondacholapuram'.

---

5 www.ariyalur.nic.in/tourist-place/gangaikonda-cholapuram/

It was inspired by a victory in a war campaign. As a symbol of the same victory, the city was established, and the temple was erected. The history of the temple cannot be fully comprehended without knowing about this war campaign, which was significant for the Cholas. For this, first, we need to know about King Rajendra Chola-I. One of King Rajaraja's queens, Tribhuvana Mahadevi, a princess of the Cher dynasty, was the mother of Rajendra (birth name Madhuranthangam or Virarajendra). King Rajendra's father, Rajaraja, wanted his son to become an excellent ruler, and this aspiration was fulfilled through his guidance. He gave Rajendra lessons in various subjects such as administration, governance and commerce. Moreover, he also taught him strategy, tactics and diplomacy. Importantly, at the age of twenty years, Rajendra was entrusted with the responsibility of an independent military campaign.

It is said that in 1002 CE, he began leading military campaigns. With his strategic acumen, military prowess and bravery, he successfully carried out campaigns independently and earned the trust of King Rajaraja. In the year 1012 CE, King Rajaraja chose Rajendra as his successor for the throne. Following this, Rajendra shared the responsibilities of governance with his father and in 1014 CE, after Rajaraja's death, Rajendra succeeded to the throne. During the next thirty years, until 1044 CE, King Rajendra reached great heights of success.

During the reign of the ambitious King Rajaraja, the Chola dynasty fought many wars. They already had great influence in the south, even conquering parts of modern-day Sri Lanka. Owing to a strong desire to conquer north India, they drew up military campaign plans accordingly. During this time, Rajendra accompanied his father on the battlefield. However, Rajaraja's attempts to expand his empire were unsuccessful due to the strong Rashtrakuta dynasty, and his dream of conquering north India remained unfulfilled during his lifetime. The opportunity to fulfil this dream came during the reign of Rajendra Chola. This opportunity arose due to a dispute over who would inherit the throne in the east Chalukya kingdom. The Chalukya king Vimaladitya's wife, Kundavai, was a princess of the Chola dynasty and also Rajendra's sister. After Vimaladitya's death, Rajaraja Narendra, son of Kundavai, ascended to the throne. However, his stepbrother Vishnuvardhan-VII declared Rajaraja Narendra's rule to be invalid and began preparations to overthrow him. He was supported by kings from Kalinga, western Chalukya, and Oda (present-day Odisha). Upon seeing this, Rajaraja Narendra sought help from his maternal uncle Rajendra Chola-I. Rajendra Chola-I sent his skilled general, Araiyan Rajarajan, with a large army to help save his nephew's kingdom. The war began. To demonstrate their power to Kalinga and Oda, who were against his nephew's reign, Rajendra Chola marched the Chola troops towards them and engaged in a fierce battle. The enemies could not withstand the power of Rajendra Chola-I's army, particularly the large armoured elephant force, and so they sought surrender. The Cholas began their expansion in north India in 1019 CE and conquered present-day eastern Bengal, Kalinga, south Kosala, Dandabhukti, and other significant states. This victorious campaign continued and they defeated the Pala dynasty ruler Mahipala in the north-east and reached the banks of the Ganga. This conquest was completed by the Cholas in merely two years. After this victory, the person due to whom this conquest had begun, Rajaraja Narendra, was coronated as the ruler of the east Chalukya kingdom and Rajendra Chola-I returned to his kingdom. It is said that by winning this war after defeating the northern kings, Rajendra brought the holy water of the Ganga to his kingdom. As a result, he was given the title 'Gangai konda', which means 'Bringer of the Ganges'. As a symbol of this significant victory, the new city of Gangaikondacholapuram was established.

While the founding of the city was connected to this triumph, there were other objectives at play as well. One important reason was to divide the concentration of power from the capital Thanjavur, which was the centre of economic, commercial and social activities. The division was necessary for further development to take place. The management of the expanded state's affairs was also made easier by this decision. This decision reflected Rajendra's exceptional skills in governance. The special feature of this city is that its development was planned by Rajendra-I with the help of experts, in an extremely organized manner, employing the principles of architecture of the time. To meet the water requirements of this large city, Rajendra also constructed a huge artificial lake called 'Chola Gangam', which can be seen even today. The lake is now known as Ponneri Lake. It is a matter of pride that this lake, which is sixteen miles long and three miles wide, is one of the largest ancient man-made lakes in the country.

UPON ARRIVAL AT THE TEMPLE

We did not even realize when we completed our two-hour journey and reached the temple. This was due to the unusual absence of shops, houses and settlements typically found around most temples. The city of Gangaikondacholapuram, which once surrounded the temple, was nowhere to be found. Unfortunately, the city no longer exists. This revered Brihadeeswara Temple used to be situated in the heart of the city that was the capital of the Cholas. It is astonishing that all the buildings and structures in the city, except for the temple, have crumbled to dust (the theories behind this have been discussed later herein). As we stepped out of the car, our eyes fell on the grand temple, which had somehow survived the sands of time. It looked nothing short of magical. It was as if someone had brought the monument from elsewhere and gently placed it there. The vast expanse of lush green and the clear blue sky above it contrasted with the striking reddish-brown colour of the artistic structure, creating a captivating sight that enchants the viewer. The three-dimensional view from up close was incredible and otherworldly.

While this temple is said to be a replica of the Brihadeeswara Temple in Thanjavur, it appears different at first glance. This is because the grand protective perimeter and the massive, ornate gopuras that are characteristic of the Thanjavur temple are not seen here. When the temple was erected, the temple had decorative gopuras and protective perimeter walls, which are an integral component of Dravidian architecture. However, centuries after their construction, they were destroyed. The destruction of the strong granite walls and gopuras was a hasty decision made by the British. In 1896 CE, when the British were constructing a dam on a nearby river, there was a dearth of granite.[6] To fulfil this requirement, the British higher-ups in the project directed the use of the granite from this temple. Accordingly, work began to extract the granite. After a few days when the local people came to know about the situation, they vehemently opposed it and took the matter to court. The court imposed a ban on the use of granite from the temple. However, by then, substantial damage was already

---

6 R. Nagaswamy, *Gangaikondacholapuram* (Archaeological Survey of India, 1970), p. 17.

done. The weakened walls and damaged gopuras deteriorated over time. Today, there is no entrance gate but on either side of where the gate would have been, one finds ruins of the granite walls and statues of the dwarapalas. However, the towering and massive dwarapala sculptures inside the temple reveal that these gatekeepers at the entrance are not the original ones.

After entering, one encounters a magnificent Nandi. However, before that, one sees the bali peetham (small platform for offering sacrifice), a typical feature of south Indian temples. The bali peetham is usually two feet in height and slightly smaller in width, with a flat base. One might think from the name 'bali', which means sacrifice, that the platform must be used for making sacrifices. This understanding is not entirely correct; the sacrifice does not refer to animal sacrifices but instead refers to the sacrifice of the five vices of human nature—lust, anger, greed, attachment and ego. The purpose of the bali peetham is to offer these vices, which often pose as roadblocks in the journey to achieving spiritual enlightenment, as a sacrifice to God. Therefore, the bali peetham serves a meaningful purpose in helping individuals to meet God with a pure mind, devoid of vices.

As is typical of south Indian temple architectural style, this temple has a tall dhvajastambha (flagstaff) and a magnificent Nandi. The Nandi here is grand and similar to the one at the Thanjavur Brihadeeswara Temple. It faces west and is about 200 metres away from the sanctum sanctorum. However, this limestone Nandi is not placed in a mandapa. This is unusual in a temple of such grandeur. The placement is deliberate and a result of the innovative and remarkable plan created by the progressive architects of that time. The placement is such that when sunlight falls on the Nandi made of limestone, it reflects on to the main Shivalinga. This way, the sanctum sanctorum, which does not have any provision for lamps, gets illuminated and helps visitors in taking darshan. The ornate Nandi statue in this temple is very impressive. Even though humans appear tiny in front of this massive Nandi statue, it remains the first choice for tourists to take pictures with. We also took pictures of it from different angles. The pictures greatly emphasized the grandeur of the Nandi.

The main temple structure is in front of Nandi. There are staircases made of stone on the left and the right side for entering the temple. There is a wall in front of the stairs so the stairs are only visible if one goes around the wall. After moving towards the main temple, one's eyes are drawn to the magnificent rock sculpture of a lion located on the right, facing northeast. The mouth of the lion is open, as if caught mid-roar. The mouth opening is big, such that a person can easily fit inside. When you look closely, you can see that the mouth has an iron grill gate inside it and steps going down. The sculpture is called Simhakeni. The staircase in the mouth of the lion leads down to a well. Although the lion statue was installed in the nineteenth century, the well itself is ancient. It is believed that the holy water of the Ganga brought after the conquest of the north was poured into this well and the ancient Gangacholam tank. According to another popular legend, in ancient times, there was a demon named Danasur who ruled over this region. He fervently wished to bathe in the holy waters of the Ganga. He devotedly prayed to the river goddess Ganga and his wish was granted when she appeared in this well. While the story is not backed by any evidence, even today, there is a tradition of using the holy water from the well for the worship of the deity.

JOURNEY THROUGH CHOLA HERITAGE

Before climbing the temple stairs, I looked at my watch and realized that there was still time for the temple to open. So we decided to take a tour of the temple premises and headed to the left, i.e., towards the southern side of the temple. One finds a beautiful, well-maintained garden here. The temple is built on a vast six-acre rectangular plot and is on the east-west axis. The temple is an excellent example of Dravidian architecture and has been designed symmetrically. The entire temple is made from granite rocks. Unlike contemporaneous south Indian temples, the shikhara of this temple used to be taller than the gopura. However, as mentioned before, the gopura of this temple has been destroyed. The construction of this temple was completed in 1035 CE. Similar to the temple at Thanjavur, the main temple structure here consists of an ardha mandapa (half-open hall) and a maha mandapa with a vimana on top of it. However, the main structure is slightly elevated. The temple has three entrances—the man entrance is to the east and the other two are to the south and north. All the doors are adorned with magnificent carvings of a pair of dwarapalas. The main temple is surrounded by five sub-temples, which are usually temples of parivar devatas (family deities). We were now facing the entrance of one of these sub-temples viz. the small Ganesha Temple situated on the southwest side was now before us. The beautiful little temple has a small mandapa with a sloping roof made of stone supported by tall stone columns and an idol of Lord Ganesha in the sanctum sanctorum.

After taking Lord Ganesha's darshan, we sat on the stairs for a while. We could see the intricately carved walls of the southern side of the main temple. The Brihadeeswara Temple of Thanjavur was built in 1010 CE, whereas the construction of this temple began

Gangaikondacholapuram Temple, Tamil Nadu

Gajalakshmi sculpture at Gangaikondacholapuram Temple, Tamil Nadu

The grand sculptures of Dwarapalas (guardians of the temple) at the south gate of the Brihadeeswara Gangaikondacholapuram Temple, Tamil Nadu

Sculpture of Chandeshanugrah at Gangaikondacholapuram Temple, Tamil Nadu

Goddess Saraswati at Gangaikondacholapuram Temple, Tamil Nadu

Side view of Gangaikondacholapuram Temple, Tamil Nadu

after the victory of Rajendra-I's expedition towards the Ganga river in the north in 1023 CE. It is said that the experts, architects and workers who built the Thanjavur Temple were involved in the construction of this temple. While Rajendra-I did build this temple by taking inspiration from the Thanjavur Temple, he had some different ideas regarding its construction. Therefore, although it is said that this temple is a replica of the temple in Thanjavur, it is unique in some aspects. The main difference is in the structure of the vimana. The Thanjavur vimana is square-shaped, with its corners gradually tapering as they rise up, culminating in a circular dome at the top, whereas the vimana of this temple is square-shaped and gradually transforms into an octagon in the middle and then into a circular shape at the top. The unique shape makes this temple appear comparatively more delicate and elegant. According to some scholars, the two Brihadeeswara temples are a symbol of the indivisible union of Shiva and his wife Shakti, with the Thanjavur temple representing Shiva (male) and the Gangaikondacholapuram Temple representing Shakti (female).

Another important difference is that the height of this temple is fifty-five metres, which is ten metres less than the Brihadeeswara Temple in Thanjavur. The temple in Thanjavur has a thirteen-story vimana, while this temple's vimana has only nine storeys. Since this temple was built later, it is certain that the height was intentionally kept lower than the other temple. Some say that King Rajendra-I purposely kept the height of the temple lower than the temple built by his father in a show of respect towards him. If we look at the life of King Rajendra-I, it is evident that he was greatly influenced by his father Rajaraja. Although it is true that the foundation laid down by his father played an important role in King Rajendra-I's path to success, Rajendra's ambition, skill in achieving his goals and his overall excellence must be credited. Known as the 'undefeated warrior', history recognizes Rajendra as a formidable king in what was Asia at the time. From the beginning of his career, he defeated the traditional enemies of the Cholas—the western Chalukyas, the Pandyas and the Cheras—and consolidated his position. Three of his military campaigns are considered very important from a historical perspective. One of these was his campaign to conquer the north mentioned above.

His first military campaign (in 1017 CE) was against Sri Lanka. This campaign was preceded by a long history of animosity between the two dynasties. To give a brief background, in 920 CE, the Pandyas and the Cholas fought a great battle,[7] in which the Pandyas were defeated. However, the Pandyas gave their crown and other treasures to the Sinhalese king for safekeeping. Even though the Cholas won the war, they felt that the Sinhalese king had helped the Pandyas cheat. In order to exact revenge, the Cholas attempted to invade Sri Lanka during the reign of King Rajaraja. However, they were unsuccessful. It was Rajendra-I who, in 1017 CE, finally succeeded in conquering Sri Lanka after a long and arduous campaign. The Cholas remained the dominant power in Sri Lanka until 1070 CE.

The later war of 1025 CE between Rajendra and the ruler of Srivijaya (present-day Indonesia) is considered remarkable. It is also noteworthy because it was the first naval battle fought and won by an Indian king. Some say that the battle was the product of a dispute that arose during the emergence of trade and commerce in the region. Since Srivijaya was located in the middle of the trade route and

---

7 www.lankaweb.com/news/items/2017/09/03/the-imperial-cholas-conquest-of-sri-lanka-dna-india/

a naval chokepoint, its king, King Sangrama Vijayatungavarman, practised naval trade monopoly. Rajendra-I started this war to keep him in check. Rajendra-I displayed exceptional bravery during this naval battle. Some scholars also theorize that this war was a war of religion. In the battle between the Buddhist kingdom of Tambralingam (a kingdom in the Malay archipelago) and the Shaivite Khmer King Suryavarman-I, Rajendra supported the Khmer king, whereas the Srivijaya ruler Sangrama Vijayatungavarman (who was a Buddhist) sided with the Tambralinga king. Rajendra was enraged by Vijayatungavarmam's disregard for the long-standing friendship between the Srivijaya and Chola kingdoms. It is said that this was one of the reasons he launched an attack against Srivijaya. In this battle, Vijayatungavarmam lost and surrendered. However, the Cholas did not establish their rule in Srivijaya. They maintained control over the politics and commerce of the region and received regular tributes from Srivijjaya for several years.

Rajendra Chola-I brought several regions under his control, including Sri Lanka, the Malay archipelago (including Myanmar, Thailand, Malaysia and Singapore), the Andaman and Nicobar islands, Lakshadweep, Java and Sumatra. Even Cambodia's Khmer rulers were influenced by him. This king who continued the legacy of encouraging arts and culture was popular among his subjects due to his good governance. His name carried weight across the Asian continent. The golden age of the Chola dynasty, which began with King Rajaraja, was taken to its zenith by King Rajendra. He was a visionary who recognized the importance of international relations, business practices and maritime dominance. Unfortunately, his achievements are not adequately recognized in history.

A GLIMPSE INSIDE

It was now four o'clock in the evening. A crowd had formed near the entrance of the temple since it was now time for the temple to open. We also stood in line to enter. When the doors opened, we walked through the grand doorway guarded by the majestic dwarapalas and entered the ardha mandapa. On either side of the path leading to the darshan area, there were two elevated open chambers. They must have been used for various purposes in ancient times. In the chambers, there are small temples of Nataraja and Devi. Further ahead was the maha mandapa. After crossing it, we entered the mukha mandapa (pavilion in front of the doorway of the temple). Pairs of grand dwarapalas can be seen here as well. When we entered, we noticed that the entrance to the sanctum sanctorum was covered by a curtain. The curtain was drawn as the pooja was going on. The biggest Shivalinga in south India was now a few feet away from us. We eagerly waited for the curtain to open. When the curtain opened and we saw the magnificent Shivalinga, we were truly overwhelmed. We kept looking at the deity of Brihadeeshwara for a long time with our hands joined. This sacred Shivalinga is four metres high and eighteen metres wide. The speciality of this linga is that it has a 'Chandrakanta' gem placed in it, which is believed to draw energy from the moon and may therefore be considered a symbol of female energy. Known as the third eye of Shiva, this gem is said to keep the sanctum sanctorum warm in winter and cool in summer.

On reaching the main temple, one can see the very prominent Suryapeeth monolithic sculpture made of stone. This sculpture, which has a square-shaped base, is divided into two parts. In the upper section, one finds a lotus in the centre, representing the sun god, with eight planetary deities surrounding it. Meanwhile, in the lower section, there is a carving of the chariot of the sun god. It was very interesting to decipher the symbolism of this carving. The chariot is pulled by seven horses, which symbolize the seven days of the week. The twelve months of the year are represented by the twelve spokes of the chariot's wheels. This intricate rock sculpture does not seem to follow the Chola art style. According to some, this sculpture is similar to Chalukya-style sculptures. It is believed that this chariot sculpture might have been brought to this temple after a victorious battle, as was the tradition at the time.

After taking darshan, there is a door towards the south side of the main hall for exiting. There is also a door towards the east side which was used by kings to enter the temple in ancient times. When we exited the hall, we were once again greeted by the sight of the magnificent dwarapalas. We walked down the numerous steps and returned to the southern part of the temple. Since we were done with taking darshan, we began walking leisurely, admiring the sculptures on the outer wall. On the southern wall, there are sculpted images of Kankalamurti, Ganesh, Ardhanarinateshwar, Dakshinamurti, Harihara and Nataraj. The variety of expressions and movements depicted in the sculptures left us amazed. We then entered the western part of the temple, that is, the rear side. In every Chola temple, there is a lingodbhava sculpture, which is a manifestation of Lord Shiva emerging from a linga. This can also be seen here. Along with that, there are sculptures of Gangadhar, Mahavishnu and Subramanya on the western wall. Moving ahead to the north, there are sculptures of Kalantaka, Durga, bearded Brahma and the fierce Bhairav with a garland of skulls. Behind them, there are two small sub-temples. One of them is dedicated to Goddess Durga and the other to Chandeswara, a Shaivite saint, one of the sixty-three Nayanars mentioned previously. Then one comes across the entrance door for kings, referred to earlier. Next to the stairs of the entrance, there is a famous Chandeshanugraha sculpture on the wall. This is an extremely beautiful sculpture of Lord Shiva that is found only in south India. It depicts an incident from Indian mythology, wherein Lord Shiva had garlanded Saint Chandesha because he was pleased with his worship and devotion. The sculpture shows Lord Shiva and Parvati seated on a pedestal, with the devotee leaning against their feet, while Lord Shiva himself is placing a garland around the head of the devotee. Rajendra Chola-I was also an ardent devotee of Lord Shiva, as demonstrated by this sculpture. It is believed that this sculpture depicts King Rajendra Chola-I's face instead of Saint Chandesha. This magnificent and intricate sculpture is a sight to behold. On the opposite wall, there is a very detailed sculpture of Gajalakshmi and Saraswati with her veena. The temple's vimana is also adorned with an abundance of sculptures and carvings. On the upper part, there are sculptures of the directional deities, the eleven Rudras and Soma. Since the vimana is quite tall, it is not easy to see these sculptures, which made me wish I had brought a pair of binoculars with me.

After observing these sculptures for a long time, we finally reached the northern end of the temple. From here, we could see the Simhakeni. Our attention was drawn to the numerous beautiful sculptures placed on an open raised platform. After the British authorities ordered the removal of stones for the construction of a dam around 1896, a small rectangular hall which was next to the outer walls of the temple, collapsed. Only the floor of the hall, i.e., the platform, remains. A large number of sculptures were placed on the platform and the rest were piled up in the corner in the overgrown grass. Some of them belonged to the time when the maha mandapa of this temple had once collapsed. The rest are said to have been found in the city of Gangaikondacholapuram. Unfortunately, these are the only remaining traces of this city, with the rest of the city being razed to the ground. It is theorized that the city was buried in the ground for many years. Two or three dynasties after the Cholas, a new colony was being established. During this time, a farmer, while digging a well, found the remains of the Chola palace at a depth of fifty to sixty feet. It was during this time that the ruins of this city came to light.

At that time, some stone inscriptions were found which speak about the city and its organized layout. The major roads, the entrances to the city, the major canals in the water system, lakes and wells are also mentioned in the inscriptions. According to the Indian archaeological department, the city was surrounded by a protective wall made of baked bricks. However, over time, due to local people taking and using these bricks as and when needed, the wall is no more. Granite slabs, wooden beams, remnants of baked brick walls, and a portion of a charming roof lined with terracotta tiles have been found in the remains of a huge Chola palace. Chinese-style wall paintings have also been found, confirming that the Cholas had strong trade relations with China. The existence of a network of roads and canals, ten temples, and evidence of the multi-storeyed houses of the rich, speak to the advanced nature of development in this city. The city was established in 1025 CE and remained the capital of the Cholas for 250 years. The coronation ceremonies of all the Chola kings were conducted in this city. So far, no one has been able to unravel the mystery behind its annihilation. However, some theories have been postulated. According to some, it may have been caused by a natural disaster. Meanwhile some contend that the Pandyas, who were traditionally considered the enemies of the Cholas, razed this city in the thirteenth century. However, it is difficult to accept this argument because the Pandyas were also Hindus and there is evidence in Chola inscriptions of them having donated to the Gangaikondacholapuram Brihadeeswara Temple. Therefore, it seems unlikely that the Pandyas would destroy the city along with its ten Hindu temples. It is also quite puzzling why the ten temples in the city were destroyed but this one was spared. It is also possible that the city may have been destroyed during the successive military campaigns of the Delhi Sultanate viz., Sardar Malik Kafur (1311 CE) followed by Khusrao Khan (1314 CE) and Muhammad bin Tughlaq (1327 CE). Even after looking into all this history, many questions remain about the survival of this temple. Whatever the reason may be, this temple still stands as a timeless beauty.

After a circumambulation of the entire temple, we again reached the Nandi. Even when the time to leave had come, my eyes could not turn away from this magnificent temple. We are so fortunate that we can still bear witness to this temple, which is an embodiment of our glorious history, unparalleled art and advanced civilization. Every time I looked at this temple, my heart filled with gratitude towards our ancestors. I kept thinking that we should honour our ancestors who built it and keep their rich legacy alive.

5

TIMELESS BEAUTY: THE ART AND HISTORY OF AIRAVATESVARA TEMPLE

The soft morning sunlight illuminated the town of Darasuram as we entered it to see the Airavatesvara Temple. The daily hustle and bustle had commenced in this quaint town near Kumbakonam. Its sleepy lanes stirred to life as the traffic steadily increased. The shops and markets had opened and were gearing up to welcome customers. As we savoured the crisp morning air coming in through the windows, our car took a turn and reached the Airavatesvara Temple complex. I fell in love with the scenery as soon as I laid eyes on it. It was stunning: there were large square expanses of greenery interrupted only by inner pathways cutting through the open spaces, and mature tamarind trees standing sentinel on the perimeter of this lush haven. I saw the robust, dark trunks of the tamarind trees bathed in golden sunlight, laden with hefty branches and lush green leaves. Through the foliage, the stone walls of the Airavatesvara Temple emerged, adorned with endearing Nandi sculptures. Our footsteps gravitated naturally towards the temple set within that beautiful landscape.

The Airavatesvara Temple is the third temple of the 'Great Living Chola Temples'. There is no definite information about when the construction of this temple began or when it was completed. However, there are references stating that its construction was initiated sometime around 1160 CE and that it took twenty years to complete. Notably, this temple was built around 150 years after the Gangaikondacholapuram Shiva Temple. The Shiva temples at Gangaikondacholapuram and Thanjavur, both built by Chola kings, showcase the zenith of Dravidian architectural and sculptural style. Given this rich historical context, our curiosity intensified as we approached this temple commissioned by Rajaraja-II, a king hailing from the same illustrious dynasty.

After exploring the outer area, we headed towards the temple and first came across the Nandi mandapa. We thought we did not see the gopuras as we had entered the temple from the non-conventional southern entrance. However, we later learnt from the locals that there used to be a gopura in the east which was destroyed. Its ruins were visible behind the Nandi mandapa. Based on the size of these remains, we deduced that the gopura must have been massive. The stone inscription at the temple mentions that the gopura was artistically adorned with sculptures. Back at the Nandi mandapa, we saw a bali peetham and a small set of steps. A unique feature of the Nandi mandapa, which we have not seen in any other Chola temple, is that it is situated within a square kunda (pool). In olden times, it must have been filled with fresh water, as suggested by the steps leading downward into it. Today, the pool has no water, except during the rainy season. Fortunately, during our visit, heavy rains in the area provided a serendipitous opportunity to witness the kunda in its original splendour. The Nandi mandapa, the Nandi, the imposing stone gateway, the lush greenery that surrounds the temple and the mirror-like reflection of all these in the water, created a scene that was truly meant to be appreciated.

A distinctive feature of the kunda is the saptaswara (seven-note) steps. Alongside the Nandi mandapa, there are seven small steps made of hard rock. When struck lightly, they produce the sound of the seven musical notes, in sequence. The mechanism behind this phenomenon raises intriguing questions about the technology employed during its creation. The curiosity surrounding the origin of the notes adds to the allure of this extraordinary feature. For safety considerations, a metal grid has been installed over it in recent times. Facing these steps lies a lotus-shaped bali peetham, with the Nandi mandapa positioned behind it. In contrast to the larger

Nandi sculptures in Thanjavur or the Gangaikondacholapuram Temple, the Nandi here is relatively smaller, complemented by a similarly modest stone mandapa. Yet, the stairs ascending towards Nandi are a spectacle in themselves. These petite and intricate steps feature sculptures depicting dancing, music and singing—capturing men and women in various joyous moods. It is akin to a preview of the vibrant scenes awaiting exploration within the temple.

Upon entering this temple, enthusiasts of architecture and sculpture will feel like they are in Alibaba's cave, surrounded by treasures. The intricate and soulful craftsmanship adorning every corner leaves visitors in a state of awe, prompting contemplation on what to explore next. While the temple may not boast the grandeur of the Thanjavur and Gangaikondacholapuram temples at first glance, a closer inspection reveals unparalleled beauty in its exquisite carvings. The twenty years taken to construct the temple does not seem like a long time when one sees the astounding sculptures within. Like the Thanjavur and Gangaikondacholapuram temples, this Shiva temple stands as a splendid example of Dravidian architecture.

LEGENDS ASSOCIATED WITH THE TEMPLE

One might be curious about the origins of the name of the Airavatesvara Temple, since it is distinct from both the Brihadeeswara temples. The Airavatesvara Temple is named after a mythological story associated with Airavata, the divine white elephant and vehicle of Lord Indra, who was born out of the churning of the ocean. According to legend, Airavata became proud of his white colour and misbehaved with Saint Durvasmuni. In response, Durvasmuni cursed Airavata to no longer be white. Repentant, Airavata came to this sacred place and performed penance to seek forgiveness from Lord Shiva. As part of his penance, he bathed in the holy pond at this location every morning. Pleased with Airavata's devotion, Lord Shiva granted him forgiveness and restored his original white colour. Airavata returned to heaven, free from the curse. The temple is thus named to commemorate Airavata's penance and the divine intervention of Lord Shiva.

There is also an interesting story about the Airavatesvara kunda associated with Yamadeva (the god of death), that tourists are often told. According to this tale, Yamadeva was cursed, and his body started burning uncontrollably. Despite various attempts to alleviate his suffering, the burning persisted. In desperation, Yamadeva took a dip in the holy water of the pond at the Airavatesvara Temple, and miraculously, his inflammation calmed down. This sacred pond came to be known as 'Yama Theertham', and a small temple dedicated to Yama can be found to the southwest of the main temple, featuring an idol of him.

To be fair, there is no evidence to support these mythological stories associated with the temple. Interestingly, during my research for this article, I came across a reference suggesting that the temple was originally known as 'Rajarajeswaram', named after the reigning king, Rajaraja-II, who commissioned its construction. Rajaraja-II succeeded his father, the Chola king Kulothunga-II, and was declared heir to the throne in 1146 CE. Despite his official rule beginning in 1150 CE after his father's death, inscriptions indicate his rule spanning from 1146 to 1173 CE. Remarkably, Gangaikondacholapuram served as the capital of the Cholas, but King Rajaraja-II displayed a keen interest in the sub-capital, present-day Darasuram, formerly known as 'Rajarajpuram', where he spent the majority of his life. Some scholars suggest that the king even relocated the capital to 'Rajarajpuram', named after himself. Rajaraja-II governed for twenty-six years, with the initial years marked by challenges and the latter half characterized by relative peace. During this period, Rajaraja-II left an indelible mark on temple architecture and art by commissioning the construction of the Airavatesvara Temple. This masterpiece continues to captivate observers with its astonishing beauty and serves as a testament to the enduring legacy of Rajaraja-II in the field of art and culture.

INTRICATELY CARVED RAJGAMBHIR TIRUMANDAPAM

Upon entering the main temple complex and reaching the first mandapa, we were immediately fascinated by the innovative architectural designs on display. This particular mandapa was crafted to create the illusion of horses pulling a chariot. Delving into the history of such architectural concepts, I discovered that about fifty years prior to the construction of the Airavatesvara Temple, the Amirthakadeswarar Temple, commissioned by Chola king Kulothunga-I in 1113 CE, also employed a similar design. However, a comparison reveals a stark contrast in complexity and grandeur between the two. While the concept was present in the Amirthakadeswarar Temple, the Airavatesvara Temple elevated it to a new level of magnificence and proportion. The desired effect of a chariot being pulled by horses is more pronounced and awe-inspiring in the Airavatesvara Temple, showcasing advancements in architectural innovation. Subsequent temples embraced the concept of a temple or mandapa being pulled by horses or elephants like a chariot. This design evolution suggests progress in architectural techniques, notably seen in later temples commissioned by Pallava kings. A strikingly similar structure can be observed in the Sun

Temple at Konark, built approximately a hundred years after the Airavatesvara Temple, further highlighting the enduring impact and evolution of this innovative architectural concept.

The distinctive architecture of the Airavatesvara Temple unfolded before us, presenting an enchanting tableau. A majestic horse, poised on its hind legs with its front legs raised in the southern direction, dominated the scene. Behind it, a grand chariot wheel added to the spectacle. To the east, steps led to the mandapa adorned with intricately carved elephant sculptures. These elephants, with uplifted trunks, intricate decorations, and a sense of dynamic movement, contributed to the temple's well-defined aesthetic.

After ascending the steps, we reached the famous Rajgambhir Tirumandapam. Our attention was particularly drawn to two remarkable sculptures on the exterior walls of the mandapa. The first depicts Nagaraja, the serpent king, with five hoods crowning its head. This human-like figure featured four arms, two of which were folded in prayer over its chest, exuding a gentle expression. The second sculpture portrays Sage Agastya in a seated posture. He is depicted beautifully, with a serene expression on his face, a withered janva (sacred thread) going across his protruding belly and hands holding a rudrakshamala (prayer beads) and a kamandalu (water pot). There is debate regarding whether this representation of Agastya belongs to the Vedic period, as numerous illustrious Agastyas were prominent in the south, leading to confusion about their identities and contributions. Shridhar Venkatesh Ketkar's Marathi encyclopaedia mentions an Agastya, who served as the guru and minister of the first Pandya king, and was a scholar of sculpture science, which suggests that this might be a sculpture of him and not the Agastya from Vedic times. Known for his text *Agastya Sakaladhikara*, Agastya laid down rules on proportions for

The Airavatesvara Temple in Tamil Nadu, viewed from the back, showcasing the Lingodbhava sculpture along with other carvings and the vibrant painting work done by the Nayak rulers

A graceful sculpture of Goddess Saraswati holding a lotus and a *kalash* (pot) instead of a veena at Airavatesvara Temple in Tamil Nadu

Intricately carved Shiva-Surya Ardhanari sculpture at Airavateshwar Temple, Tamil Nadu

The striking facade of the Airavatesvara Temple in Tamil Nadu, featuring a unique architectural style, a chariot hall and exquisite carvings

The north mandapa of Airavatesvara Temple in Tamil Nadu which contains sculptures of Shaivite saints and inscriptions detailing important events in their lives

Beautiful carvings on the columns at Airavateshwar Temple, Tamil Nadu

idols, a legacy incorporated into subsequent sculpture texts like *Kasyapiya, Saraswatiya* and *Anshuman-Vedkalpa*. These guidelines, still considered valuable by sculptors today, contain details on sculpting the sixteen forms of Lord Shiva, reflecting the significance of the Shaivite tradition during that period. It is plausible to assume that the inclusion of the Agastya sculpture in the temple could be a gesture of gratitude and respect toward him by the sculptors, acknowledging his contributions to the field of sculpture science.

The Rajgambhir Tirumandapam boasts a remarkable array of 108 columns, renowned worldwide for their intricate miniature carvings. The mandapa begins with a slightly elevated open area, resembling a porch, which is balanced by twelve stone columns. Along the outer side of this space, eight pillars showcase sculptures of the mythical creature 'Yali' (Vyal) near the ground. Yali, a fantastical being amalgamating various animals, is a common motif in south Indian temples, symbolizing the harmonious integration of diverse animal characteristics. In this instance, the yalis, known as gajvyal, exhibit a distinctive structure, featuring the trunk of an elephant and a body resembling that of a lion. During our visit, a local guide explained each organ in the yali structure in detail, revealing a composition that includes several animals—lion, elephant, dragon, eagle, bull and pig. Notably, all eight yali sculptures on the columns share a common design, only with differentiated tails. These yalis are believed to have been crafted with the specific intent of safeguarding the temple by warding off evil forces.

Among the twelve pillars, the four central pillars stand out for their exceptional and distinct carving patterns. These pillars narrate stories from the Skanda Purana in a serialized form, depicted in mesmerizing miniature carvings. The carvings unfold a sequence of events, including Daksha's yajna, the humiliation of Shiva during the ritual, Parvati's courageous entry into the fire, the ensuing war between the deities and Shiva's ganas, Parvati's intense penance to win Shiva's favour, the marriage ceremony of Shiva and Parvati attended by Vishnu and Brahma, and the musicians of the wedding procession. The detailed carvings vividly bring these scenes to life, capturing the speed, emotion, and overall atmosphere of each moment. Observing these miniature sculptures, I found myself completely engrossed in the narratives, appreciating the skill and artistry of the sculptors who brought these stories to life in stone. In that moment, I could not help but offer a heartfelt mental bow of admiration and gratitude to the talented craftsmen behind these living carvings.

Upon entering, we encountered a spacious hall adorned with numerous carved stone columns, spanning twenty-three metres in the southwest direction and a little over twenty-one metres in the east-west direction. As we gazed into the interior, the mandapa appeared to be a space seemingly designed for artistic performances and enjoyment. Some scholars share a similar hypothesis, suggesting that this temple was not primarily constructed as a centre of trade and commerce, unlike the temples at Thanjavur and Gangaikondacholapuram. Instead, it was envisioned as a centre for entertainment and stress relief.

This purpose is affirmed by the choice of images carved into the pillars of the mandapa. The Chola kings' tradition of promoting various arts, including the royal patronage of Bharatanatyam, a dance form, is reflected herein. The temple features the 108 mudras (hand gestures) of this dance art engraved on the pillars. Some miniature sculptures, as tiny as a finger, are a must-see. These include a dancing Ganesha, Shiva and Parvati engaged in a relaxed interaction, and the depiction of Gajasamhara. The Gajasamhara sculpture, also known as Gajasuravadh, narrates the tale of Shiva vanquishing an asura named 'Neel', who assumed the form of an elephant. In the tale, after slaying the asura, Shiva wears the elephant skin. In this miniature sculpture, Shiva is portrayed with eight hands, wielding a damaru (drum), khadga (sword), trishul (trident) and gajacharama (elephant hide). Parvati, positioned beside Shiva, appears frightened by his rudra (fierce) form, while holding the infant Kartikeya. This particular depiction has garnered the attention of sculpture scholars, who acknowledge it as a remarkable piece of art within the temple.

Entering the hall, we found ourselves in awe, unsure of where to direct our gaze amid the overwhelming beauty. The intricately carved roof added to the visual splendour. Notably, this space houses miraculous sculptures, playing with the illusion of vision. One such example is the portrayal of a female acrobat viewed from multiple perspectives. Initially, she appears seated, but upon closer inspection, her body seems to be kneeling on the right side, her legs neatly folded. Intriguingly, she presents a different stance when viewed from the left side. In a delightful twist, the fourth perspective showcases the same woman engaged in exercise, with her body weight supported by her arms and both legs raised from behind. These optical illusions add a layer of marvel to the artistic wonders within the hall, leaving its viewers immersed in the skilful craftsmanship and the playful magic of visual perception. There is also another impressive and elaborate sculpture called Vrishabha-Kunjaram in the Shilpaslesh style,[8] which is found on the temple wall. It features a single face with a twist: an optical illusion whereby on one side it is an elephant and on the other it is a bull.

---

8 Shlesh is a Sanskrit word. Its literal meaning in English is 'pun'. It is used to describe the sculpture when one can derive from different angles two or more figures.

KING RAJARAJA-II'S LEGACY

This mandapa was given the name Rajagambhir, after a title given to King Rajaraja-II. At the beginning of his reign, he faced many challenges and had to assert his dominance. Prior to his rule, the Chola empire had expanded greatly, and he was tasked with maintaining its control. He successfully rose to this challenge. It is said that this king did not get a chance to show much valour on the battlefield during his reign because not many major battles or wars were fought during his tenure. However, the king did have to deal with rebellions and discontent on several occasions. This benevolent ruler prioritized the welfare of his people, ensuring a just and humane response to difficult situations, earning respect across society, the military and the administration. His historical legacy is defined by his exceptional management skills.

The dissatisfied Pandyas posed a notable challenge for Rajaraja-II. Long-held resentment stemming from previous defeats fuelled civil unrest during his reign. The Cholas, right from Aditya Chola (871 CE to 907 CE), had consistently subdued the Pandya kings, keeping them under their influence. However, the Pandyas, unwilling to concede defeat, began strengthening their armies in the twelfth century. During Rajaraja-II's rule, this discontent erupted into a wave of civil unrest within the Pandya territories under Chola control. Simultaneously, the Cheras of Kerala also opposed the Cholas. With timely and effective measures, Rajaraja-II managed to bring the situation under control, restoring peace. Throughout his reign, he quelled rebellions and maintained control over the territories, administration, army, and maritime trade routes. His adept leadership ensured stability and prosperity in the Chola empire during a time of regional challenges.

The reign of Rajaraja-II was characterized by affluence, prosperity and stability, fostering a continued tradition of promoting art, literature and architecture. The Airavatesvara Temple stands as a testament to this flourishing cultural era. Exploring the royal Tirumandapam, I marvelled at the intricacy of each column, where different images were meticulously engraved. Not only were the columns adorned with unique carvings, but the borders and surrounding elements also exhibited a variety of artistic expressions. Comparing the grandeur of the Airavatesvara Temple with the Thanjavur and Gangaikondacholapuram temples proved to be a mistake, as the current state of the Airavatesvar Temple does not fully represent its historical magnificence. Inscriptions reveal that the temple complex originally consisted of seven mandapas, seven internal roads and seven consecutive fortifications. The existence of ruins at a distance from the temple further confirms this historical layout. However, similar to the fate of Gangaikondacholapuram, the destruction of other structures around the temple is evident though the reasons remain unclear. Some scholars expound that the reasons might be the same as those of Gangaikondacholapuram. Reflecting on the information from inscriptions about the temple's original vastness, I was struck by the grand scope of Rajaraja-II's temple construction. Historical records portray Rajaraja-II as a benevolent and generous king, known for his charitable acts and regular donations to temples. His gentle and generous disposition, coupled with a strong inclination towards religious works, is evident in his frequent visits to temples in Thanjavur, Chidambaram, Kanchipuram, Srirangam, Trichy and Madurai, where he consistently made contributions. Additionally, his generosity extended to temples in Kerala, where he regularly offered donations.

TEMPLE INTERIORS

As we made our way toward the next mandapa, the striking sculptures on both sides of the entrance immediately captured our attention. These magnificent sculptures, characterized by intricate details and depicted with a satisfied expression on their faces, beckoned us to pause and appreciate their artistry. Among the four sculptures, one depicts the Shaivite saint Kannapa—a figure whose life underwent a profound transformation through unwavering devotion to Lord Shiva. Kannapa, once a bandit, dedicated himself entirely to the lord, reaching the pinnacle of surrender by even offering his own eyes to Shiva. In this sculpture, Kannapa is portrayed holding a bow and wearing leather footwear. Another sculpture features Nandikeshwara in Anjalimudra—a posture conveying reverence. The third sculpture portrays the goddess Ganga standing while holding a lotus in one hand and a vessel in the other. While interpretations of the goddess vary among scholars, some suggesting she is Annapurna and others Tribhuvaneshwari, the sculpture's aura of mystique remains appealing. The fourth sculpture in this series portrays Saraswati Devi in a seated position. Interestingly, unlike typical Saraswati sculptures, this one is not depicted holding a veena in her hand.

After seeing these sculptures, we entered the ardha mandapa. Upon entering, we encountered a serene space adorned with thirty-six stone pillars, deliberately free of carvings. The absence of embellishments serves a purpose—to facilitate a calm and focused state of mind as visitors proceed to the main mandapa for the darshan of the deity. The simplicity of the ardha mandapa was designed to avoid distractions and encourage a tranquil environment for worship.

Continuing our journey, our attention was drawn to the famous sculptures of the gatekeepers, Chanda and Munda, crafted from gleaming granite. These sculptures were skilfully carved to evoke a sense of fierce intensity. Our eyes lingered for a moment on these exquisite sculptures before coming to rest on the Shivalinga in the sanctum sanctorum. The square-shaped sanctum sanctorum of twelve metres houses the Shivalinga. The atmosphere within was serene and uplifting, enhanced by the fragrance emanating from the Shivalinga, which was decorated with large flower garlands, and illuminated by oil lamps that cast a warm glow. As we stood in the peaceful presence of the Shivalinga, the overall ambience was one of calm and joy, creating a profound and contemplative experience.

In accordance with Dravidian architecture, the spire or vimana atop the garbhagriha of this temple soars to a height of twenty-five metres, comprising five distinct levels. A unique feature of this temple is the absence of a circumambulation path around the garbhagriha. The relative lack of crowds during our visit allowed us to immerse ourselves in the tranquil surroundings.

During our time at the temple, the priest offered us holy water and shared with us some details about the temple. He said that the temple, despite its historical significance, does not consistently draw large crowds. This apparent lack of visitors may be attributed to factors such as the absence of a direct transport system and the misconception that it bears similarities to the Thanjavur temple. While this might hold true for some Indian tourists, foreign visitors visit frequently. During our visit, we encountered a large group of tourists from Japan and China. Witnessing their appreciation for the temple's exquisite architecture, unparalleled stone sculptures and its nearly 800-year-old history, instilled a sense of pride within me. However, as an Indian, the apparent indifference displayed by some of our fellow countrymen towards their own cultural heritage was disheartening.

After visiting the temple, we stepped outside to circumambulate around the temple. As we strolled along the southern part, our attention turned to the beautiful sculptures embellishing the temple walls. The Chola kings, staunch followers of Shaivism, played a pivotal role in the dissemination of this sect's beliefs within society, which is reflected in the temple's design. Notably, the base of the temple (upapeetha) features depictions of the sixty-three Shaivite saints known as Nayanars. Their stories are showcased, in a beautiful narrative, through seventy-three sculpted panels. These sculptures are rare and found only in a few temples. As we observed the intricate details, the experience was akin to watching an animated film. However, those familiar with the stories behind the saints' sculptures will feel a deeper connection. Moving to the north side of the temple, we explored the verandahs. One finds 108 stone inscriptions here, out of which ninety inscriptions recount pivotal events in the lives of the Shaivite saints. Each saint is commemorated with their own sculpture. One of the stone inscriptions notes that King Rajaraja honoured the singers who sang compositions by these devoted saints, regularly bestowing them with gifts.

A tangible representation of the aggressive spread of the Shaivite sect is embodied in the form of Sharabheswara Dev, whose small temple stands within this temple complex. The statue of Sharabheshwar, an incarnation of Shiva, evokes imagery reminiscent of the Narasimha incarnation of Vishnu. He is portrayed as having a fierce lion face and the body of Garuda, with multiple arms vanquishing Narasimha resting on his lap; it appears a fearsome sculpture. As the story goes, even after the demise of Hiranyakashipu, whom Vishnu killed in the Narasimha avatar, Narasimha retained a ferocious demeanour, instilling terror among the people. In response, Shiva assumed the Sharabheshwar avatar, a form even more formidable, and subdued Narasimha. While significant differences of opinion exist between the Shaivite and Vaishnavite sects regarding the authenticity of this narrative and the avatars of Lord Shiva, the Sharabheshwar incarnation stands as a witness to the diverse journeys undertaken by both sects. Remarkably, there are only two or three statues depicting this incarnation throughout India, making the presence of Sharabheshwar Dev in this temple complex a unique and rare sighting.

THE TEMPLE'S BEAUTY AMIDST MODERN CHALLENGES

King Rajaraja-II had a profound appreciation for beauty and aesthetics, apparent in the construction of this temple. The attention given to the temple's aesthetics is evident in its magnificent design, showcasing an innovative plan that was carefully implemented. The outer perimeter of the sanctum sanctorum is surrounded by an impressive 3.66 metres-long granite slab and a delicate 25.40 centimetres-long wall running alongside the slab. Along the short wall, there are several circular, deep-shelled areas, serving a unique purpose. They are part of an ingenious plan whereby water would be released in the strip formed between the slab and the wall, which was illuminated by night lights within the circular areas on the side wall. To manage excess water in the belt, particularly during rainy periods, small shafts shaped like Nandis were strategically erected on the wall. These miniature Nandis, resembling a lotus in form, efficiently channelled excess water out of their mouths. Regrettably, no intact Nandi sculptures adorn the wall today, with only broken pieces remaining. Despite the current state, the creativity and artistic vision employed for beautification during that era are admirable. The successful completion of this ambitious temple project is a testament to the unwavering willpower and determination of King Rajaraja-II.

A brief visit to this temple is insufficient to discover all its treasures. Each facet of the temple is intricately woven into the fabric of our extraordinary history and culture, demanding a nuanced understanding. There is no information centre or official guide at the temple. While some priests make efforts to provide guidance, securing such assistance is often a matter of chance.

Another disheartening aspect is the susceptibility of the temple premises to waterlogging when there is rainfall, even if it is minimal. The absence of an effective drainage system leads to prolonged flooding of the temple during the rainy season. The flooding makes it difficult to access the small shrines adjacent to the outer wall, dissuading many tourists from exploring these areas. While not versed in the technical intricacies, our first-hand experience during a bout of rain revealed the deficient drainage system. The entire temple's architectural splendour, as elaborated above, was observed through stagnant water, and even the sculptures on the temple's foundation were submerged. The thought of these remarkable sculptures remaining submerged for an extended period during the rainy season evoked a sense of profound sadness in me.

Rajaraja-II ruled his kingdom until his demise in 1173 CE. Since his sons were still young, he declared Rajadhiraja Chola-II as his successor in 1163 CE. In the subsequent years, Rajaraja-II's son, Kulothunga-III (1178 CE to 1218 CE), ascended the throne, ensuring the continuity of the dynasty. Inscriptions on the temple bear witness to its renovation during Kulothunga-III's reign. The state of preservation of this temple is attributable to it remaining within Hindu territory—first with the Cholas for an extended period and subsequently with the Pandyas and Nayaks. Painting work in certain parts of the temple dates back to the Nayaks' era, showcasing their contributions to the temple's preservation. Inscriptions further reveal the enduring legacy of patronage, noting that even during the Chola period, the Pandyas made donations to this venerable temple.

The external walls of this temple serve as a canvas for intricate miniature sculptures, offering a visual feast of scenes from diverse aspects of life. From lively depictions of festive occasions, complete with dancing and singing, to finely detailed miniature figures portraying humans, animals and nature, the craftsmanship is unparalleled. The sculptures vividly capture delight, excitement and laughter, evoking joy in the observer.

Among the numerous sculptures dedicated to Lord Shiva, a standout panel depicts the burning of Manmatha, showcasing unmatched detailing, lines, curves and emotions. Moving towards the north, panels narrating episodes from the Ramayana, particularly the Vali–Sugreeva war and Lord Rama's involvement, are noteworthy. One also finds depictions of certain uncommon subjects, such as a friend aiding a woman in labour, people enjoying animal fights, and instances of domestic violence. A panel illustrating a woman tightly gripping her husband's hair as he screams in pain is routinely pointed out by local guides whereas another panel depicting a woman quietly enduring a beating by a man does not receive much attention.

The exterior walls also feature large sculptures. Most of these are crafted from black basalt which creates a striking contrast against the pale granite walls. Notable sculptures include Nagaraja, Agastya, standing Ganesh, Lingodbhava, Bhairav, Nritya Martanda, Shivsurya Ardhanari, Mahishasuramardini, and Dhanvantari. As we walked along the walls observing these, we reached the entrance of the temple again. The flagpole near the entrance has two sculptures on either side, which I initially thought were sculptures of Kuber but later found out were those of Padmanidhi and Shankhanidhi.

When we entered the temple, our historical journey unfolded, traversing through the twelfth century of the Chola period, delving into the ancient Shiva era on the Tirumandapam chariot, and finally, witnessing pivotal events from the Ramayana. We seamlessly reconnected with the social life of the Chola period. Although the enchanting journey had concluded, the awakened sense of respect and pride for our ancestors, instilled by this temple, would endure in our minds indefinitely.

6

TRACING THE ANCIENT ECHOES OF HINDU CULTURE IN CAMBODIA

Cambodia (or Kamboj), located over 2,900 kilometres from India in Southeast Asia, boasts a fascinating historical connection with the Indian culture that once thrived in this distant region. Notably, Cambodia is home to Angkor Wat, the world's largest temple dedicated to the Hindu god Vishnu, along with numerous Hindu and Buddhist temples. Remarkably, these grand temples, now globally admired, remained hidden for 400 years till the mid-nineteenth century. These 900-year-old temples were shrouded by remote and dense forests.

The discovery of Angkor Wat's crumbling structure by a chance observer in 1860 brought Cambodia into the global spotlight. Subsequent exploration revealed a network of temples, including Angkor Wat, which had been concealed for centuries. This sparked extensive research that unveiled forgotten truths of the past, prompting questions about the arrival of Hinduism and Buddhism in the region, the prolonged obscurity of these ancient temples, and the gradual disappearance of the urbanization that once showcased artistic heritage through temple construction. Motivated to find answers to these questions, we decided to visit Cambodia. While Angkor Thom and Angkor Wat are the major tourist attractions, Cambodia hosts numerous other Hindu and Buddhist temples. We planned an eight-day trip to try to see as many temples as we could. During our stay in Siem Reap over the Diwali holidays, we sought answers to our questions through various avenues. Our experiences and findings during this exploration are shared here, shedding light on the mysteries surrounding Cambodia's rich cultural history.

The turning point that brought the Hindu and Buddhist temples to light after four centuries of obscurity unfolded with the arrival of French colonists in the sixteenth century. They eventually asserted full control over the area by the eighteenth century. The pivotal moment, however, occurred in the 1860s when French naturalist Henry Mouhot, residing in the region, ventured into the Cambodian forests in pursuit of a butterfly. As he entered the remote woodlands, he was astounded by an unexpected sight. Amidst towering trees and tangled vines, the pinnacle of the Angkor Wat temple emerged, a testament to the artistic prowess of stone construction. Henry Mouhot, deeply moved by this encounter, documented his experience, describing the magnificent structure. Tragically, within a year, Mouhot succumbed to a venomous insect bite. It was not until 1863 that his article on Angkor Wat was published. The moment it reached London and Paris, it triggered a sensation. Archaeologists, photographers, and researchers from around the globe flocked to Cambodia, eager to authenticate the remarkable find. Numerous organizations actively began engaging in research, with some individuals devoting their lives to the study of these temples. While Mouhot is credited for introducing this hidden gem to the world, evidence suggests that some Westerners had visited the site earlier. A Portuguese adventurer explored the area as early as the sixteenth century and had left written accounts. However, for reasons unknown, it did not garner much attention at the time.

The exploration and preservation efforts for these temple complexes commenced in 1863, following the publication of Henry Mouhot's article. However, it was much later, in December 1992, that UNESCO bestowed 'world heritage' status upon the site, propelling the conservation work into full swing. A startling discovery was made when NASA employed satellite technology in its investigation of the site. The temple of Angkor Wat was surrounded by traces of an ancient city, its expanse far surpassing previous estimations. This revelation, pre-dating the era of industrialization, indicated the existence of the world's largest city at that time. The satellite imagery revealed a meticulously planned network of canals and roads, suggesting an exceptionally advanced city with an estimated population of around one million people. Traces of numerous temples from that period were also identified. Subsequent use of laser scanning technology unveiled the presence of another town called Mahendraparvata, located forty kilometres north of Angkor Wat. The findings showcased the remarkable sophistication and scale of these ancient urban settlements.

The credibility of this information was proved by two crucial discoveries—1,200 inscriptions spanning the sixth to fourteenth century and the diary entries of a Chinese diplomat. These inscriptions were composed in Sanskrit and Old Khmer. They posed a challenging task in translation, a feat accomplished in eight parts by the French scholar George Cœdès.[9] Additionally, the diary entries of Zhou Daguan, a Chinese officer who resided with a local family here for eleven months in 1296 CE, provided valuable insights into the social life and the reigning king of that era. These offered a guiding light for further research.

A glimpse into the region's history provides insight into who was responsible for establishing such an advanced civilization. 'Kamboj' is an ancient name. In the Khmer language, Cambodia is still referred to as 'Kamboj'. The valley of the Mekong river once housed an advanced culture, now known as the Khmer culture, thanks to the Khmer empire that once ruled the region. However, even

---

9 Amir D. Aczel, *Finding Zero: A Mathematician's Odyssey To Uncover The Origins Of Numbers* (Palgrave Pan, New York, 2015), pp. ix, 95, 96, 174–178, 219.

before the Khmer empire, the ancient Hindu kingdom of 'Funan' existed in the southern part of Cambodia from the first century CE to 613 CE. The original name of this kingdom might differ, as the name 'Funan' was given by the Chinese. Intriguingly, there is a tale surrounding the adoption of Hinduism and culture by the state, yet consensus is lacking on whether this story pertains to the birth of the Khmer dynasty or the era of Funan.

As the story goes, around 200 BCE, an Indian Brahmin named Kaundinya came to this region accompanied by a group of people. The inhabitants of the area were known as the Nagas. It is recounted that the princess of the Naga people fell in love with Kaundinya, leading to his becoming the son-in-law of the land. Subsequently, Kaundinya ascended to the throne and imparted Hindu culture to the country. The capital of the state, Vyadhpur, was founded by Kaundinya. Inscriptions found in the region corroborate the narrative that Kaundinya married a Naga princess. Chinese historians have also extensively written about Kaundinya. Since that time, Indians seem to have held a significant influence in the region.

During this period, India experienced a remarkable era of prosperity under the rule of the Vakataka, Pallava and Gupta kings. The nation thrived with active trade, flourishing enterprises, and advancements in agricultural techniques. India's sophistication at the time is evident, as the rulers of Funan actively sought the expertise of Brahmins from India, suggesting that India was likely more advanced than other parts of Asia. These Indian Brahmins played a crucial role in the administration and artistic endeavours of the Funan kingdom. Excavation evidence and aerial photographs reveal the existence of canals and agriculture during this historical period. Trade through Cambodia's ports also prospered during this period.

The Indian influence in the region was primarily through maritime trade. However, as the vassal 'Chenla' of the Funan empire gained strength, the empire began to decline in the mid-sixth century. Amidst the chaos in the Funan dynasty in the early seventh century, a figure named 'Kambu', who had arrived from India, assumed control. From that point forward, the country became known as 'Kambuj', later evolving into the name 'Cambodia'.

The era of Funan, which embraced Hindu religion and culture, was until 681 CE. Bhavavarman and Mahendravarman fostered the development of Cambodia during their reigns. Mahendravarman's son, Ishanvarman, expanded the state's borders and forged diplomatic ties with India and Champa (present-day Vietnam then under Hindu rule). Successive rulers, Bhavavarman-II and Jayavarman ruled Cambodia. However, after 674 CE, the province faced invasion by King Shailendra of Java.

In the ninth century, the region once again fell under the control of the Khmer empire. The credit for reclaiming control of Cambodia from the king of Java is attributed to the formidable ruler Jayavarman-II (who reigned from 802 CE to 850 CE). By vanquishing rival kings in the region, he declared himself 'Chakravarti' (ideal universal ruler). To safeguard the kingdom, Jayavarman-II reportedly invited the Brahmin scholar Hiranyadam[10] from India, and together, they performed tantric rituals towards this end. During Jayavarman-II's reign, several significant traditions emerged, including the establishment of the 'Devaraja' cult by scholar Hiranyadam. This cult was adopted as the royal religion of Cambodia. Following coronation, kings were prefixed with the title 'Devaraja', signifying their role as representatives of God. The people, displaying deep

---

10 www.ams.com.kh/khmercivilization/detail/8361

love, devotion and faith, regarded the king as akin to a deity. This sentiment is evident in the construction of monumental temples despite the challenges and the absence of modern technology, and is a testament to the immense faith placed in the king. Under King Jayavarman-II's rule, the kingdom expanded from east to west, prompting changes in the capital's location. The king shifted the capital first to Kuti,[11] then to Hariharalaya, and finally to Amarendrapur[12] near present-day Angkor. It became customary for each new monarch to establish a new city and declare it the capital upon ascending the throne.

The construction of temples was initiated under the reign of Indravarman (who reigned from 877 CE to 889 CE), the succeeding monarch in this dynasty. His rule, characterized by stability and peace, allowed the state to focus on vital aspects such as irrigation, agriculture and trade. The resulting wealth was directed towards temple construction, including the establishment of the Preah Ko and later the Bakong Shiva temples. These temples, adorned with intricate carvings, still stand today at erstwhile Hariharalaya, situated fifteen kilometres from the Angkor Wat main temple. The golden age of the Khmer empire is said to have begun with Yashovarman (who reigned from 889 CE to 910 CE), the son of King Indravarman. Yashodharapura, the capital he established, is considered to be the first city in Cambodia. Proficient in Hinduism and Sanskrit poetry, Yashovarman extended royal patronage to numerous scholars. This era witnessed unprecedented progress in Hinduism, art and literature, establishing Angkor as a prominent

---

11 www.bharatdiscovery.org/india

12 www.heritageindiaimages.com/angkor_wat.php and www.bharatdiscovery.org/india

centre for religion and culture. Sanskrit was officially adopted as the state language. About 600 inscriptions out of the 1,200 discovered in the temple complex are in Sanskrit, proving its widespread use. These inscriptions, following precise grammar rules, begin with homage to the temple deity and subsequently praise the temple's founder (the king). These beautiful inscriptions in poetic style were written in the time of King Rajendravarman after he ascended the throne in 944 CE. They are predominantly dedicated to the praise of Lord Shiva.

As time went by, the form of inscriptions began to change. The alphabet in fifth-century inscriptions resembles the script of the 'Pallava' kingdom in south India. Some inscriptions at the temple complexes are in Khmer and in verse form. Some are lists detailing items owned by the temple deity and its devoted servants. Here, the term 'servant' conveys the meaning of a 'devotee' rather than someone employed by the temple.

Two pivotal figures in the later period of the Khmer empire were King Suryavarman-II (who reigned from 1113 CE to 1150 CE) and King Jayavarman-VII (who reigned from 1181 CE to 1218 CE). They are renowned for creating two of the most breathtaking architectural marvels on earth, namely Angkor Wat and Angkor Thom, respectively. Before delving into their accomplishments, it's essential to explore the central concept of Hinduism, elucidated through metaphor, which serves as the foundation for the construction of ancient temples in Cambodia. According to this belief, gods reside on Mount Meru, the centre of the universe connected to heaven. Four mountains surround Meru, and they, in turn, are encompassed by the kshira sagara (ocean of milk). The architectural design of most Cambodian temples, resembling pyramids or mountains, symbolizes these metaphors. The temple-peak of the main deity represents the Meru mountain, while the peaks of the other four deities symbolize the four surrounding mountains. The gopura and circumambulation paths represent the mountains encircling Mount Meru, and the vast water-filled trenches surrounding the temple depict the kshira sagara. Additionally, ledges resembling serpents, are erected around some temples, and scenes depicting samudra manthana (the churning of the ocean) are evident in numerous temples.

ANGKOR WAT

Angkor Wat, meaning the 'City of Temples' in the Khmer language, is home to the world's largest Vishnu temple. It was constructed in the twelfth century by King Suryavarman-II. This ambitious ruler demonstrated his prowess from a young age, building his army as a teenager. With this army, he overthrew his uncle from the throne and seized control of the kingdom. Records indicate the presence of Indian priest Diwakar Pandit at his coronation in 1113 CE. Later, King Suryavarman-II expanded the kingdom's borders, even extending his influence into Vietnam. His reign was marked by efforts to foster art and commerce by establishing friendly relations and trade ties with powerful nations like China. Notably, he maintained friendly relations with the Chola dynasty in southern India. There are historical records of valuable diamonds being gifted to King Kulothunga of the Chola dynasty by Suryavarman-II. However, even before Suryavarman-II, the Khmer empire had robust diplomatic and political connections with the Chola dynasty.

The preceding king, Suryavarman-I (who reigned from 1006 CE to 1050 CE), had a very cordial relationship with King Rajendra Chola-I, who held sway over all of Asia. Seeking military aid from

King Rajendra in a battle against the King of Tambralinga (a kingdom in the Malaya Peninsula), Suryavarman-I emerged victorious with Chola support. The Chola army remained stationed in his state for an extended period. History also mentions that Suryavarman-I sent a chariot as a gift to King Rajendra.

Before Suryavarman-II, all the Hindu kings of the Khmer empire were Shaivites, worshipping Shiva. Consequently, only Shiva temples were built until that period. Suryavarman-II was the first Khmer king to recognize Vishnu as the royal deity, embracing Vaishnavism as the royal religion, and erecting the magnificent Vishnu temple now known as Angkor Wat. Originally named 'Vishnulok', the temple underwent a transformation in the thirteenth century when Buddhism gained rapid traction in Cambodia. Subsequent kings adopted Buddhism as the royal religion, converting the temple into a Buddhist one. An idol of Lord Buddha was installed in the main sanctum, while the original splendid Vishnu idol was relocated to a circumambulation path.

The quest for undiscovered temples in Cambodia started with the iconic Angkor Wat after Henry Mouhot first laid eyes on this temple, shrouded in dense forest. Despite claims that Angkor Wat had returned from complete obscurity, locals argue that it was never entirely unknown, serving as a place of worship for various communities over time. When the locals were probed about the structure's history, numerous legends came to light. A notable one suggests that the gods themselves erected the temple overnight for their own dwelling. Another tale attributes the construction to Indra, the king of the gods, who built it for his son. While these legends may lack historical accuracy, they reflect the extraordinary nature of the temple's construction.

To appreciate the genius behind the Vishnu temple built by Suryavarman-II, which stands as a masterpiece challenging the norms of its time, let's briefly delve into the structure of the temple. Standing on an impressive 400–450 acres of land, the grand temple is a symbolic masterpiece, meticulously designed with the metaphor of Mount Meru in mind. This huge portion of land served as the capital of the Khmer kingdom, encompassing the temple at its centre. The temple features three circumambulation paths. The length of the temple complex measures 1.5 kilometres east to west and 1.3 kilometres north to south. The outer circumambulation path along the external protective wall measures 1,024 metres on two sides and 802 metres on the remaining two sides. Surrounding the temple is a moat, 190 metres wide, four metres deep, and extending for a total of approximately five kilometres, consistently filled with water. This trench served a dual purpose: symbolic and practical.

The ingenious water management system utilized the waters of the Mekong river, flowing from China and Tibet, and the Tonlé Sap, an expansive shallow lake at the heart of Cambodia. Cleverly incorporating these water sources, the system facilitated agricultural practices and supplied water to the city. The Mekong river is linked to the Tonlé Sap, allowing water to flow from the river to the lake during floods and back to the river as the flood recedes. This water, channelled through canals connected to trenches, was also utilized for the irrigation of the paddy fields outside the town. The comprehensive scheme aimed to regulate water levels, preventing excessive rise during the rainy season and ensuring sufficient levels in the summer. This strategic water management enabled thrice-a-year paddy cultivation, making the region self-sufficient in food production and contributing to the state's wealth through surplus trade. The success of this water supply scheme is regarded as pivotal in supporting the ambitious urbanization and the realization of colossal projects, such as the construction of large-scale temples, at the time.

Bridges gracefully span the vast trench on the east and west sides, providing access to the breathtaking temple beyond the town. As we crossed the bridge, the magnificent temple unfolded before us. Passing through the three-door gopura, we encountered a stone-built verandah. Beyond it lies a pathway flanked by library and dispensary buildings on either side. One finds a library seemingly outside every temple in Cambodia. Adjacent to this pathway is a charming pond adorned with blooming lotus flowers.

Continuing along the path, we arrived at a circumambulation route featuring doors in four main directions. The western door hosts the grand original eight-handed Vishnu statue. This idol was originally housed in the sanctum sanctorum of the main temple. During the excavation of the site in 1943, two crystals and two gold leaves were discovered. It is possible that they were placed there as sources of energy.

On the second circumambulation path, we encountered circular carved stone pillars on one side and bas-reliefs (uthavashilpa) adorning the wall opposite them. These bas-reliefs not only depict historical processions and celestial events including the battle between gods and demons, but also offer a glimpse into the royal court of King Suryavarman-II. Notably, this is the first time a Khmer dynasty king is showcased in bas-reliefs.

While exploring the temple complexes in Cambodia, a distinctive and enchanting bas-relief frequently catches the eye—the depiction of apsaras (celestial nymphs). Whether portrayed individually or in groups of three, these graceful and alluring dancers are intricately carved on pillars and ceilings throughout the temple. Notably, the portrayal of apsaras underwent changes over time as the influence of art evolved within the state. In the early days, akin to Indian carvings, the nymphs were depicted with a slightly curvier physique, a characteristic that transformed in later temples. The pinnacle of apsara bas-reliefs is reached in the Angkor Wat temple. Here, one can marvel at the beauty of at least 1,000 nymphs.

Ascending a set of steps and traversing the third circumambulation path, a majestic sight unfolds—the towering, square, pyramid-like main temple. Encircling this imposing structure are narrow steps. Most of these steps have deteriorated with time due to which ascent is only allowed from the east side. As you ascend, the main temple, featuring a square circumambulation path and adorned with four gopuras on each corner, comes into full view. The shikhara of the main temple stands tall at an impressive height of sixty-five metres.

One unique feature of this temple is its west-facing orientation, deviating from the usual east-facing direction of Hindu temples. This departure might be attributed to the association of the god Vishnu with the western direction in Hinduism.

The tomb of King Suryavarman-II is also situated within this temple. From a different perspective, this could explain why the temple was designed in alignment with Mount Meru. It is said that the king wanted the construction of this temple to be completed before his death so it could serve as his tomb. The 'Devaraja' (deity king) wanted to make Mount Meru, the abode of the gods, his final resting place due to his desire to reach moksha (freedom from the cycle of birth and death). While the construction could not be completed before the king's death, taking thirty-seven years to complete, the king's wishes were respected. Accordingly, the tomb of the king is placed beneath the main temple.

The temple has several magnificent verandahs and thousands of bas-reliefs portraying narratives from the Mahabharata, the churning of the ocean, the story of Aniruddha and Usha, the Ram–Ravana war, and various events from the Ramayana. The towering temple peak, intricate carvings, and the precision in construction, defying even modern techniques, leave a profound impact when witnessed firsthand. In essence, this temple stands as a celebration of religion, art, architecture and authority, showcasing the profound cultural and spiritual richness of the Khmer empire.

ANGKOR THOM: THE BAYON BUDDHIST TEMPLE

While Bayon is primarily a Buddhist temple, it has been included here due to multiple reasons. First, it has a connection to the central idea of Mount Meru mentioned earlier. Second, some of the bas-reliefs carved in this temple depict Hindu deities, reflecting the influence of Hinduism on the region before the construction of this Buddhist temple. Third, it was converted to a Hindu temple at one point of time. These matters are discussed in detail later herein.

The spread of Buddhism in Cambodia began during the later part of the eleventh century. There are differing views on the origin of Buddhism in this region, with some attributing its promotion to Buddhist monks from Sri Lanka and others believing it was introduced from India. King Jayavarman-VII, the creator of Angkor Thom, was a devoted follower of Buddhism. Some posit that he was initially a Hindu and that his adoption of Buddhism was influenced by his sister-in-law, Indradevi. Indradevi, a woman of sharp intellect who mastered Sanskrit, had converted to Buddhism. She played a significant role in teaching women in temple schools and had a profound impact on Jayavarman's wife, Jayarajdevi. After Jayarajdevi's untimely death, King Jayavarman-VII married Indradevi, who then actively assisted the king in the affairs of the kingdom. It is said that under Indradevi's influence, King Jayavarman-VII embraced the Mahayana Buddhist sect.

Ascending the throne at the age of sixty, King Jayavarman-VII, a mighty ruler, demonstrated his prowess by conquering traditional enemies, particularly the Cham. He won the hearts of the people through numerous philanthropic endeavours. His reign was marked by the construction of roads, canals, temples, rest houses and artificial lakes. During his rule, King Jayavarman-VII established 102 hospitals for the well-being of his subjects. This compassionate and tolerant Buddhist king extended his respect to both Shaivite and Vaishnavite sects. In honour of his mother and father, he erected the Ta Prohm and Preah Khan temples. Subsequently, he commissioned the construction of the Buddhist temple 'Bayon' for himself.

There are varying interpretations regarding the purpose behind the construction of the Bayon Temple. While some suggest that it was built based on Queen Indradevi's strong desire to create Buddhist temples, others argue that, like many kings in the region, King Jayavarman-VII aimed to establish a temple that would serve as his eternal resting place. Another perspective posits that these temples were not intended for public worship but rather as palaces for the gods to reside in. This perspective proposes that the temple was constructed so that the deity would be pleased with the king and his family and bestow his blessings upon them. Scholars note that, despite the grandeur of the temples, the narrow circumambulation routes limit the possibility of large gatherings and processions. It is possible that some temples like Ta Keo might have been constructed solely as residences for the gods, as there is no apparent entrance for worshippers.

The Bayon Temple's fame worldwide, attributed to its grand carved faces, is matched by Angkor Thom, the meticulously planned capital city built by King Jayavarman-VII. This city, considered a marvel of its time, was designed with the citizens' convenience in mind. It has become a focal point of interest for tourists, scholars and researchers from across the globe.

Angkor Thom, translating to 'Great City', lived up to its name by being one of the finest cities of its era in terms of expansion, planning and civic amenities. It spans an area of 360 acres. It is fortified by a robust perimeter wall made of laterite stone, measuring eight kilometres in length and three metres in width. Despite damage over time, remnants of this wall are still visible today. On the outskirts of the town is a 100-metre-wide trench that surrounds the fortification, symbolizing kshira sagara. A bridge allows passage across the trench and entry into the city. The bridge is decorated with a depiction of samudra manthana on both sides, with gods and demons shown churning the ocean using the Vasuki serpent as a rope. On one side of the bridge, there are fifty-four gods and on the other side, the same number of demons. The faces of the gods are shown to be calm and the demons are portrayed to be angry. The gods and demons standing in line, gripping Vasuki, bring to mind an image of a spirited game of tug-of-war. The original idols have undergone some damage and subsequent restoration.

Upon crossing the trench via the bridge, we entered the city through one of the four gopuras. The gopuras, symbolizing the mountain range near Mount Meru, have large faces carved on them facing each of the four main directions. The city has a total of five entrances: one each in the north, south and west directions, and two in the east. Among the eastern entrances, one is named the Victory

Gate, historically serving as the entry point for victorious armies into the city.

The grand roads emerging from the entrances in these four directions lead to the Bayon central temple. It was originally named 'Jayagiri'. Unlike other temples in Cambodia, Bayon lacks a perimeter wall and trench around it, as the city itself is enclosed by a protective wall. After ascending a slight incline, we reach the Bayon Temple. This grand temple is structured across three floors, featuring eight entrances with gopuras adorned with four faces each. A gallery of bas-reliefs graces the path to the sanctum extending over the first two floors of the temple. The first floor of Bayon is adorned with carvings depicting historical events and daily life scenes. There are also carvings of market scenes emphasizing the significant role of women, aligning with the historical accounts of Chinese diplomatic officer Zhou Daguan. Notable engravings include depictions of rooster battles, naval encounters with the Cham and Champa kingdoms, and grand victorious processions, complete with bearded Chinese soldiers with their hair in a bun. Engaging with these sculptures allows the imagination to wander into the social life of that era, creating a captivating experience that can make one forget the passing of time, even under the intense rays of the sun overhead.

Similar to other temples, the Bayon Temple's bas-reliefs also showcase numerous apsaras. The second floor, or inner gallery, features carved mythological scenes from Hinduism, including depictions of Ravana, Garuda, and the trinity of Brahma, Vishnu and Mahesh. The third floor boasts towers adorned with numerous faces, with a total of 216 faces intricately carved into the temple's structure. There is no consensus among scholars as to whom these faces belong to. Some scholars believe that the faces belong to

Avalokeshwara or Padmapani Bodhisattva, while others say they are the faces of King Jayavarman-VII, who saw himself as a divine figure due to his title as 'Devaraja'. The primary temple, symbolizing Mount Meru, stands at a height of forty-three metres. It initially housed a meditating Buddha idol in its sanctum sanctorum, which is no longer present. Following Jayavarman-VII, his son Indravarman took charge of completing the temple project.

The construction of both the entrance of the city and this temple places significance on the number nine. In the ocean-churning scene depicted on the bridge over the trench, there are fifty-four gods and fifty-four demons. The sum of five and four equals nine, and the total number of gods and demons is 108, with the sum of one, zero and eight equalling nine. The Bayon Temple itself has fifty-four towers, and 216 faces are engraved on it. Once again, the sum of these numbers equals nine. The spiritual significance of the number nine is acknowledged in both Hinduism and Buddhism.

King Jayavarman-VIII, a staunch Hindu following Shaivism, converted all the Buddhist temples into Shiva temples during his reign. It is reported that the meditating Buddhist statue in the Bayon Temple was removed at that time. After Jayavarman-VIII, the Khmer empire began to decline. His successor, his son-in-law who embraced Buddhism, could not restore the empire to its former strength. The region was plagued by frequent battles and revolts. Since there was no primogeniture system, whereby the oldest son succeeded to the throne, every ambitious and powerful relative lay claim to the throne. Disputes persisted among the king's family members, leading to civil unrest throughout the Khmer empire's history. The dynasty witnessed conflicts over the rule of eleven out of the total twenty-seven kings. Despite the challenges, the construction of temples continued from the eighth century until the thirteenth century. The process of constructing these temples, considered almost impossible given the lack of modern technology, remained a mystery for a long time. However, bas-reliefs carved in the temples provided a systematic explanation of the construction process, unexpectedly unravelling the mystery for researchers.

The construction of the temples primarily employed materials such as brick, sandstone and laterite. In the eighth and ninth centuries, bricks were the predominant material, with surviving examples like the Preah Ko and Bakong temples showcasing their durability. Notably, the Preah Ko Shiva Temple features remarkably well-preserved, beautiful Nandi idols. In later years, the main structures of the temples were constructed using laterite. Laterite, rich in iron content, starts soft as clay but hardens when exposed to sunlight and air. However, due to its porosity, it was not suitable for the visible, carved portions of the temples. Therefore, sandstone, known for its softness, was used for the intricately carved sections. The temples would first be built with laterite and later adorned with carved sandstone. For the construction of the arches, the original stones were shaped by rubbing them against each other and then stacked, using sandstone for this purpose. Similar to the Hemadpanthi style of architecture, no adhesive has been used to keep the stones in place. A lock and key mechanism is used between stones to maintain structural integrity.

The stones used in the temple were quarried from Mount Kulen, located thirty kilometres to the north. A thoughtful plan was devised to facilitate the transportation of these massive stones. The Mekong river, originating from Mount Kulen, and an extensive network of canals were ingeniously used to transport the stones. The circular holes visible in the large square stones of the temple were created for ease of transportation and construction. These holes were made

The gopura at Bayon Temple, Cambodia, featuring faces looking towards the four cardinal directions, symbolizing the mountain ranges surrounding Mount Meru

Angkor Wat, Cambodia

Naval battle bas-relief at Bayon Temple, Cambodia

The Banteay Srei Temple, Cambodia, with its intricate and beautiful carvings on red sandstone which likely earned it the title 'Jewel of Khmer Art'

The ruins of Ta Prohm Temple, Cambodia, famous for being featured in the movie *Tomb Raider*

Bayon Temple, Cambodia

The Bakong Shiva Temple in Cambodia, considered the first Khmer temple-mountain made of sandstone at Angkor

in the stones during their extraction from Mount Kulen. To lift and move the heavy stones, bamboo or wood was inserted into the holes, and water was poured over it. The wood would swell, securing itself tightly in the stone, making it more manageable for labourers to lift and transport. The same technique was used during the temple's construction for smoothening the surface of the stones. The wooden stems were used as handles to lift stones and rub them together with water applied in between.

During the eight days of exploration, we visited many temples and witnessed their spectacular beauty. However, when they were initially discovered, many of these temples were in a dilapidated state. One Hindu temple, Beng Mealea, built by Suryavarman-II and known as the 'Lotus Pond', can still be seen in such a state today. It has a unique beauty, set amidst a magical environment of tall trees, birds and open air. While extensive reconstruction and conservation efforts have been carried out on all the temples, preserving them in their original form, the untouched beauty of Beng Mealea is a must-see due to its distinctive charm.

Several countries have contributed to the conservation efforts of these temples after they were declared UNESCO World Heritage sites. France took the lead in these efforts and continues to provide help in this respect. India, too, has actively participated in these preservation projects. Specifically, India has taken on the responsibility of conserving the Ta Prohm Temple, nestled amidst the towering trees and famously featured in the movie *Tomb Raider*. This temple, constructed by Jayavarman-VII, holds immense appeal for tourists. It was heartening to see the Indian flag proudly displayed on the information board outside the temple. Despite the increased crowds due to its popularity, conservation work at Ta Prohm was in full swing during our visit.

Banteay Srei, a tenth-century Shiva temple, stands out as particularly enchanting among the many beautiful temples in the region. Originally named Tribhuvanamahesvara, the size of this temple makes it look like a small-scale replica of the grand temples in this temple complex. It boasts exquisite red sandstone carvings, earning it the titles of 'precious gem' and 'jewel of Khmer art'. It is located at a distance from the main temple complex. Notably, this temple was not commissioned by a king but was built by Yajnavaraha, the minister, advisor, and priest of King Rajendravarman-II. The intricate bas-reliefs at Banteay Srei depict various deities, the dancing forms of Shiva, the battle between Vali and Sugreeva, and unique scenes like the fire in Forest Khandava, showcasing a rich tapestry of stories. Bas-reliefs like Kansavadh, Jarasandvadh, Hiranyakashipuvadh, etc. also can be seen. Amusingly, André Marlowe, a minister in the French de Gaulle cabinet, enamoured by the beauty of these bas-reliefs, was caught trying to pick up three of them from the temple.

Despite the advanced culture, flourishing arts and prosperous urbanization, the region eventually became deserted. The questions surrounding the abandonment of this once-thriving area and the temples for 400 years remain unanswered. The mystery of why people left and why these temples were forgotten continues to intrigue visitors. While reliable answers remain elusive due to the lack of information between 1300 and 1600 CE, there are multiple hypotheses regarding this mystery.

As previously discussed, the affluence of this state thrived due to an intricate network of lakes and canals. The network fostered prosperity, abundant food supplies, and a flourishing trade that contributed to the treasury's wealth. One potential factor for the desertion of this region could have been a growing population, prompting the need to expand agricultural lands to sustain growing food requirements. Consequently, widespread deforestation of Kulen Mountain and other open areas likely occurred for agricultural activities. The river originating from Mount Kulen initially fed the city's water needs, but the extensive tree clearing may have led to substantial silt and soil flow, potentially obstructing the canal's drainage. Neglect of this water supply system during crucial monitoring periods could have disrupted daily life, triggering migration. Additionally, the deforestation's impact on the weather might have resulted in irregular rainfall, causing either excessive precipitation or water scarcity, potentially prompting inhabitants to abandon the region. Another consideration could be the ongoing religious conversions at the time. Initially rooted in Hindu principles, the region transitioned to Buddhism, with successive kings adopting different sects such as Theravada or Mahayana. This constant religious flux, dictated by the reigning king's beliefs, might have generated distrust among the populace, though this argument seems somewhat weak. A fourth possibility is that the plague which originated in China around 1330 CE, may have spread to these areas and caused widespread casualties. The possibility of migration due to foreign invasion is also hypothesized.

There are very few traces of the advanced civilization that once flourished here. Records of a Chinese diplomat note that the houses of common people were made from wood and therefore might not have left visual evidence of their settlement. Thankfully, the stone temples endured the test of time, facilitating the tracing of the rich history of this region to the present day.

In the sixteenth century, the region fell under French colonial occupation. The area later experienced a harrowing genocide from the 1970s to the 1980s, marked by power struggles following independence from France. The bitter memories of the intense persecution suffered by their ancestors linger painfully among the local population. Pol Pot, a leader with staunch socialist ideologies, orchestrated the killing of an estimated 1.4 million to 2.2 million people, constituting 25 per cent of Cambodia's population.[13] The casualties escalated further during the war against Vietnam. Regrettably, during this tumultuous period, the ancient temples served as military camps, and extensive minefields were laid around them, rendering the area hazardous for habitation. Even today, some areas are deemed unsafe, including the Lotus Pond, which is now marked with warning signs about the planted mines. During this period, temple conservation efforts were also prohibited.

After a prolonged period of strife, peace was eventually restored in the country after 1980. Today, Buddhism predominates as the country's religion, embraced by 97.1 per cent of the population, with Islam and Christianity representing the remaining religious affiliations.[14] Tourism has emerged as a crucial source of income for Cambodia. While tourists from around the globe flock to explore the Hindu temples, the number of Hindus officially residing in the country, which once boasted a rich and thriving Hindu culture, is nearly non-existent today.

During my exploration of the temple complexes in Cambodia, I found myself in a unique state of contemplation. On one hand, the awe-inspiring accomplishments in art, architecture and engineering captivated me. Simultaneously, the historical backdrop of perpetual conflict, religious conversions and brutal genocide exposed the

---

13 'Demographic Expert Report' (2009, E3_2413_EN), p. 16.

14 www.nis.gov.kh/nis/Census2019/Final%20General%20Population%20Census%202019-English.pdf

manifestations of ego, authority and power in the human psyche, prompting deep reflection. Witnessing the gradual erosion of a culture that had thrived and been widely embraced for centuries was indeed disheartening. In Hinduism, the trinity of Brahma, Vishnu and Mahesh symbolizes the cycles of creation, preservation and destruction—the fundamental laws governing the universe. The Hindu culture in Cambodia is no exception to this universal truth.

7

A VERITABLE REPOSITORY OF ART: THE CHENNAKESHAVA TEMPLE

A thousand years ago, in the region of present-day Karnataka, Jain Guru Sudatta and his pupils visited the Vasantika Temple nestled in the dense jungle at Angadi. All was well until a sudden disturbance disrupted the peace. The guru located the source of this disturbance—a tiger crouching in the bushes, poised to attack. Realizing the gravity of the situation, the guru swiftly handed over his stick to his favourite pupil and commanded *'Hoy ... Sala.'* In ancient Kannada, 'Hoy' meant to strike, and 'Sala' was the name of the pupil. The pupil immediately obeyed his guru's order and struck the tiger dead.

The Sala in this tale is considered to be the founder of the Hoysala dynasty, which ruled over Karnataka for over 300 years. There is no way of ascertaining whether there is any truth to the above folktale since it is set over a thousand years ago. However, it is linked to the Hoysala dynasty due to two reasons. First, the name of the dynasty 'Hoysala' is said to be derived from the order given by the guru. Second, the royal emblem of the Hoysala dynasty is the image of a young man attacking a tiger.

During the period from 1026 CE to 1343 CE, the Hoysala dynasty governed what is now Karnataka, a small portion of Tamil Nadu, Western Andhra Pradesh, and parts of Telangana. The kingdom's prosperity and stability fostered a golden age of arts, literature and culture. The kings and the queens of this dynasty were connoisseurs of art. Some queens were skilled artists themselves. Historical sources record that art was indispensably and intrinsically entrenched in their society. The dynasty contributed tremendously to the developments in the field of art as they were patrons of various art forms such as dance, sculpture and architecture. Today, this dynasty is renowned for their brilliant and distinctive temple architecture and outstanding sculptures.

We were on our way to visit the famous Chennakeshava Vishnu Temple at Belur in the Hasan district of Karnataka, built by King Vishnuvardhan from this dynasty. Our journey from Mumbai to Bangalore and then to Hasan had been arduous, but the anticipation of witnessing the temple overshadowed any lingering fatigue. Since winter is considered the best time to visit, we planned our trip in December. When we arrived at Belur, the streets were bustling and the atmosphere was cheerful. The crisp morning air was refreshing and the pale yellow gopura of the temple, before us, was gleaming in the golden sunlight. The groups of people gathered near the stone fortification around the temple seemed to highlight its grandeur.

The five-storied gopura of this temple is known as 'Rajgopura'. The walls of the gopura are made of stone and its peak with lime and bricks. The peak is adorned with sculptures of gods and deities, especially Lord Vishnu. After admiring the beautiful sculptures on the gopura, we entered the temple. As mentioned previously, a different style of temple architecture developed during the Hoysala dynasty which was not fully Dravidian nor fully Nagar (a style popular in north India). This new style, while heavily influenced by Dravidian temple architecture, was a hybrid form of temple architecture known as Vesara, popularly known as Hoysala. Badami's Chalukya dynasty built Vesara-style temples as early as the tenth century. It is said that the Hoysala-era temples were inspired by these.

The Chennakeshava Temple premises are quite vast, spanning 135 metres from east to west and 120 metres from north to south.[15] Apart from the main temple, the premises contains other temples

---

15 Ramanujapuram Narasimhachar, *The Kesava Temple At Belur* (Indological Book Corp., New Delhi, 1979).

such as Soumyanayaki (Lakshmi) Temple, Ranganayaki Temple, Kappa-Chennigaraya Temple, Virnarayana Temple, a kitchen, a water tank and a mandapa for public ceremonies. Upon entering the temple, one is immediately struck by the vastness of the sprawling temple premises. On the right, one sees a rectangular water tank with stone steps on each side for entering. The tank used to be known as the Vasudeva Kunda, as evidenced by the ancient stone inscription there. The kitchen, mandapa and other structures are on the left and the main Chennakeshava Temple is straight ahead. As we embark on a journey to explore the temple's rich heritage and cultural significance, it is imperative to reflect on the legacy of the Hoysala dynasty, which built over 1,500 beautiful temples such as this one, during their reign.

There is no consensus among historians about the origin of the Hoysala dynasty. According to some scholars, they originated in Malnad, Karnataka, while others say they were descendants of the Yadavs from the north. In the treatise *Maharashtra Sanskruti*, historian P.G. Sahasrabuddhe propounds that the Hoysalas were a branch of the Yadavs from Devagiri.

However, amidst this divergence of opinions, one undisputed fact is that the Hoysalas initially served as provincial governors of the Chalukyas. The earliest record of this dynasty dates back to 950 CE. Arekalla, Maruga and Nripa Kama-I are mentioned as the first notable leading figures of this dynasty, followed by the very important Nripa Kama-II. Nripa Kama-II established a formidable army and cemented the Hoysala name as an important dynasty. Nripa Kama-II's son, Vinayaditya, ascended to the throne, with historical records naming him as 'Sala's son Vinayaditya'. This led historians to conclude that Nripa Kama-II was likely the first Hoysala king, given his pivotal role in shaping the dynasty's trajectory. Nripa Kama-II amassed great military power, swiftly making the Hoysala empire an influential and fearsome one. This may be the reason he is widely considered the forefather of the Hoysala dynasty.

After Nripa Kama-II, King Vishnuvardhana is considered the most important figure of this dynasty. He had an ambitious dream to free the Hoysalas from Chalukya control and was able to make it true to some extent. It was during King Vishnuvardhana's reign that the empire truly flourished—politically, culturally, and even in terms of military power. After King Vishnuvardhana defeated the mighty Cholas and conquered Talakad, he began expanding the empire. This king, who reigned for a long sixty-year period from 1108 to 1152 CE, also built the Chennakeshava Temple. The temple construction began in 1117 CE and took 103 years to finish. During this period, three generations of Hoysala kings contributed to its construction. Today, much of our knowledge about the Chennakeshava Temple's origins and history is derived from the astounding 118 stone inscriptions found within its precincts. Dating from the twelfth to the eighteenth century, these inscriptions offer invaluable insights into the temple's construction, the workers involved, charitable contributions, renovations, and other pertinent details.

TEMPLE DESIGN

One of the special characteristics of this temple is its unique star-shaped layout, a departure from the conventional rectangular or square temple designs. The distinct star shape becomes immediately apparent upon laying eyes on the temple. To us, it looked like a jewel being presented on a velvet tray, more so due to the jagati. The jagati is the three-foot-tall raised platform surrounding the temple. The jagati is also unique to Hoysala temple architecture. Instead of the traditional circumambulation path which only goes around the sanctum sanctorum, the jagati goes around the outer walls of the entire temple. The reason for constructing the jagati could be to exhibit the stunning sculptures and sculpted panels carved into the outer walls of the temple.

The temple hosts an extensive collection of sculptures. The carving work on the sculptures is unimaginably intricate, a feature of Hoysala sculptures. The remarkably minute carving-work is made possible by the use of soapstone as material for the sculpture. This stone, while malleable and soft when freshly quarried, gradually hardens as its exposure to the environment increases. King Vishnuvardhana engaged many skilled architects and craftsmen for the construction of this temple. However, the architects primarily in-charge were the father-son duo of Dasoja and Chavana.[16] It is said that they hailed from the Chalukya capital city Shimoga's Baligav region.

When one gazes at the temple, its uniqueness is striking due to the absence of two significant temple features: the shikhara and vimana. While the temple does not have a peak today, historical records indicate that it once possessed one, which was constructed from a combination of wood, lime and bricks. However, the passage of time took its toll on this structure, leading to its gradual deterioration. While the temple was renovated multiple times, and the peak continued to disintegrate, due to which attempts to restore it were abandoned. Some sources say that the peak was removed during conservation efforts for the temple.

On our way to the temple, our gaze fell upon the deepa stambha (lamp pillar) to our left. Crafted from a single slab of granite, this

---

16 www.karnatakatourism.org/tour-item/beluru/ and www.hassan.nic.in/en/tourist-place/chennakeshava-temple-belur/

remarkable pillar stands tall at a height of twelve metres. It is placed simply on a star-shaped platform without any support. The pillar is still standing, having withstood natural forces for over a thousand years. The pillar, supported only by the law of gravity, is popularly known as 'gravity pillar' among tourists. Over time, the corners of the pillar have become worn out where they touch the ground. Tour guides are often seen amusing crowds of tourists by performing a trick in which they slide a piece of paper under one corner of the pillar and retrieve it from the opposite side. We, too, enjoyed the playful demonstration before continuing towards the temple.

There is a captivating story linked with the construction of this temple. While the Hoysalas were originally from the Jain sect, they built Hindu temples on a large scale. There is no clear answer as to why. One theory suggests that they were extremely tolerant of other religious sects while another proposes that the mighty King Vishnuvardhana from this dynasty had become a Vaishnavite. To understand the reason for his conversion, one must consider the general situation at that time. When Hoysalas were ruling over (modern day) Karnataka, the Cholas reigned over (modern day) Tamil Nadu and a large part of the neighbouring area. From the very beginning, the Chola kings were Shaivites. Due to their devotion to Lord Shiva, they built countless beautiful sculpture-studded Shiva temples. These temples also contained idols of Lord Vishnu, an indication of the Chola's open-mindedness towards other sects.

In the Chola kingdom, in (modern day) Tamil Nadu, a great Vaishnava saint Ramanujacharya was born in 1017 CE. He was a proponent of the Vishishtadvaita Vedanta theory, which upholds the belief that all diversity ultimately stems from a fundamental underlying unity. Residing in Srirangam, which is in present-day Tamil Nadu, he spread Vaishnavism on a large scale. However, the

Chola king in power then, King Kulothunga-I (1070 CE to 1120 CE) was a fervent Shaivite. The zealous Shaivite king's extreme measures, including discarding an idol of Lord Vishnu into the sea, created an environment that was hostile to Vaishnavism. Some pupils of Saint Ramanujacharya had to face physical torture due to their practice of Vaishnavism (one finds mention of this in historian K.A. Nilakanta Sastri e *The Cholas*).[17] This prompted Saint Ramanujacharya to flee Srirangam and seek refuge in the Hoysala kingdom.

At that time, the ruling king in Karnataka was Jain king, Bittideva. Upon learning of the saint's arrival, the king visited the saint and paid his respects. Impressed by the saint's brilliance and wisdom, he decided to embrace Vaishnavism and learn from the saint. Upon conversion, he changed his name from Bittideva to the name he received from the saint, Vishnuvardhana. Some accept the theory of the king's conversion while others do not, claiming that the king was agnostic. Some scholars propose that the king built the Vishnu Chennakeshava Temple in honour of his guru, Saint Ramanujacharya, after becoming a Vaishnavite. It is also theorized that the temple was built under the supervision of Mudaliyandan, Ramanujacharya's sister's son, who was also his pupil. Apart from this temple, King Vishnuvardhana also built five Vishnu temples at five different locations. Popularly known as the Panchanarayana region in Karnataka, these temples are at Belur, Talakadu, Melukote, Thondanoor and Gadag. Out of these, Ramanujacharya resided in Melukote for twelve years. After King Kulothunga-I's reign ended, Saint Ramanujacharya returned to Srirangam. (While some historical references mention King Kulothunga-II instead of King Kulothunga-I, it is likely an erroneous reference since King

---

17 www.en.wikipedia.org/wiki/K._A._Nilakanta_Sastri

Kulothunga-II's reign was from 1133 CE to 1150 CE while the saint was born in 1017 CE and died in 1137 CE.)

Upon reaching the temple, we encountered a two-tiered staircase—leading first to the jagati and then ascending to the mandapa. Positioned at the beginning of these staircases, on both sides, are small sub-temples complete with peaks. Nine such Vishnu temples can be seen here. As we ascended, the stone statue of the Hoysala dynasty's royal symbol, gleaming in the sunlight, caught our eye. Flanking the entrance were statues depicting ferocious tigers being slain by a young man—Sala. Having familiarized ourselves with the story, witnessing these sculptures with the knowledge of how it came to be, added a deeper layer of significance.

Scholars remain divided on the reason behind the choice of this symbol as the Hoysalas' royal emblem. Some attribute it to the Sala and tiger story, underscoring the symbolic victory over the threatening tiger. Others propose a connection to the Cholas, suggesting that the tiger represents the Chola dynasty, as their flag featured a tiger. In this interpretation, the symbol represents the defeat of the Cholas by King Vishnuvardhana. Some also believe that the temple itself was erected to commemorate the Hoysalas' triumph over the formidable Cholas. Another perspective posits that the construction celebrated the successful resistance against Chalukya annexation.

The Chennakeshava Temple is constructed in the 'ekakuta' type of temple construction, featuring a single deity and sanctum sanctorum.[18] The temple layout comprises the mandapa, antaral (space between the mandapa and the sanctum sanctorum), and

---

18 www.wikipedia.org/wiki/Chennakeshava_Temple,_Belur#

Marichika the huntress at Chennakeshava Temple, Karnataka

Small shrines dedicated to Vishnu flanking the main temple steps of Chennakeshava Temple, Karnataka

Intricately carved Makartoran above the door of sanctum sanctorum at Chennakeshava Temple, Karnataka

Darpan sundari apsara holding a mirror at Chennakeshava Temple, Karnataka

A graceful sculpture of a beautiful Madanika in a 'tribhang' pose, engrossed in playing a musical instrument at Chennakeshava Temple, Karnataka

East gate of Padmanabhaswamy Temple, Kerala

The lake and gopura of Padmanabhaswamy Temple, Kerala

the sanctum sanctorum. Approaching the navranga mandapa,[19] we encountered three entrances on the east, north and south, each adorned with a makara torana, a distinctive feature of Hoysala temples.

The toranas, characterized by incredibly intricate carvings, display two makaras facing each other. The makara, an imaginary creature amalgamating features of seven animals, serves as the vahana of Hindu god Varuna. It has the body of a boar, the legs of a lion, the face of a crocodile, the trunk of an elephant, the eyes of a monkey, the ears of a cow and the tail is the extravagant plumage of a peacock. The carving of the plumage occupies a major part of the sculpted panel. Carvings depict Varuna and his consort Varuni seated on the makaras' backs. The central space of the toranas portrays significant scenes such as Vishnu–Lakshmi or the slaying of Hiranyakashyapu. Surrounding the scene in an arch-like formation are carvings of the ten avatars of Lord Vishnu.

Beyond the makara toranas, the doors feature additional exquisite artwork. Notably, sculpted panels showcase the figures of Madan or Manmanth on one side of the door and his beloved wife Rati on the other. The Madan–Rati pair symbolizes the feeling of lust, and their separate placement on either side of the door signifies a call for devotees to leave such feelings outside before entering the temple to worship Lord Vishnu.

---

19 It is called navaranga because the central ceiling of the madapa is divided into nine parts, each one differently carved. The navaranga roof consists of sixteen squares, nine in the sabha mandapa and the remaining seven in the extension near the eastern entrance. These are all carved, each different, each with nature motifs and Hindu theology symbolism embedded.

Two other sculpted panels near the entrance offer glimpses into historical events. The panel on the left portrays the court of King Vishnuvardhana, with the king bearing a sword, and seated alongside his first queen, Queen Shantala Devi—a talented dancer, knowledgeable individual and influential figure. Accompanying them are lady attendants, the king's guru, likely Ramanujacharya in padmasana (lotus pose), his pupils, and ministers. While the pupils and ministers are on the same side of the sculpted panel, one can easily identify the difference between the two because of the clothes and jewellery worn. Meanwhile, the panel on the right depicts the court of King Vir Ballala-II, the adored grandson of King Vishnuvardhana. It captures the king, queen, attendants and court attendees. King Vir Ballala-II played a pivotal role in realizing his grandfather's dream of freedom from Chalukya annexation, and was one of the most significant figures from the Hoysala dynasty.

As I observed the sculpted panel portraying King Vir Ballala-II's court, the historical narrative behind it came to mind. Vir Ballala-II succeeded his father Narasimha-I (who reigned from 1152 CE to 1173 CE), who was deemed an unimpressive ruler. Displeased with his father's governance, Vir Ballala-II initiated a coup against him with the support of regional chieftains, ultimately ascending to the throne. He then carefully monitored the regional chieftains to tamp down any greed for power. During his reign (1173 CE to 1220 CE), Vir Ballala-II emerged as a powerful, ambitious and remarkable king, focusing on expanding the kingdom through military campaigns.

Vir Ballala-II achieved notable victories against the Yadavs of Devagiri, the Kalachuris in the south, Pandyas of Madurai, and Chalukyas in the west. He also took control of the declining Chola empire. During the battle between the Cholas and Pandyas, he helped the Cholas win by sending an army led by his son, Narasimha. After this battle, the king received the title of 'Cholarajyapratisthacharya' meaning the king who has re-established the kingdom of Chola. He also held the titles of 'Hoysalachakravarti' (The Hoysala Emperor) and 'Dakshinachakravarti'(The Emperor of the South). Although most of the king's time was spent on military campaigns, Vir Ballala-II devoted attention to artistic endeavours, overseeing the construction of over 100 Vaishnavite and Shaivite temples, popularizing the 'Vessar' style of architecture. In folklore, he is credited with founding the present capital of Karnataka, Bengaluru.

Vir Ballala-II's reign marked a cultural zenith, with its contributions to literature in the elevation of the regional language, Kannada. He is considered by some historians as the most influential figure from the Hoysala dynasty, and his era is often regarded as the golden period of the Hoysala dynasty. His significant contributions include completing the construction of the Chennakeshava Temple. The navranga mandapa of this temple was initially open on three sides. During Vir Ballala-II's reign, the sides were closed with beautifully carved net-like panels. Today, while devotees cannot get the same light and access, these beautiful panels, on which are carved stories from the Puranas, are one of the popular attractions at the temple.

We entered the navranga mandapa while looking at the pair of Manmanth–Rati. We marvelled at the stone pillars, which were gleaming as if they had been mirror-polished. The mandapa boasts forty-eight pillars, each with a unique pattern. Some are so intricate that it seems impossible that they were made without machine assistance. The Narasimha sthambha, a pillar embellished with minute carvings, drew our attention. It is said that the pillar supposedly rotated using a ball-bearing mechanism during the temple's peak era, but this later stopped working. Due to this, today, one cannot witness the magical rotation of this stunning stone pillar. The ceiling of the mandapa showcases magnificent carvings, including a masterpiece depicting Trimurti, the trinity of Lord Brahma, Vishnu and Mahesh. Among the Hoysala temples, this temple continues to be an active place of worship, with idol worship, poojas and festivals celebrated to this day.

As the temple had been open for quite some time, the crowd of devotees swelled, prompting us to postpone our exploration of the intricate stone pillars. Instead, we decided to proceed to the sanctum sanctorum for darshan. The entrance to the sanctum sanctorum features delicate carving work, adorned with a makara torana depicting Lakshmi–Narayana. Beautiful carvings of Jaya and Vijaya, serving as dwarapalas, welcomed us—a traditional sight in Vishnu temples.

Passing through the adorned entrance, our gaze focused on the main idol of Chennakeshava. Mounted on a three-foot-tall platform, the six-foot idol has four arms holding a shell, chakra, gada (weapon) and a lotus flower. The space behind the idol is also decorated with exquisite and delicate carvings depicting the ten avatars of Vishnu. Intricate ornaments, proportionate to the idol's size, and the long slender fingers of the deity captured our attention. It became apparent why the locals affectionately refer to the deity as Chennakeshava, as 'Chenna' translates to beautiful. While the locals may have named the idol as such, enamoured by its beauty, the original name is Vijayanarana, as noted in a stone inscription.

The deity is accompanied by Goddess Bhudevi on one side and Goddess Shridevi on the other, though their sculptures are comparatively smaller, in order to draw focus to the main deity. Both goddesses, while identical in height, have distinctly carved facial features. According to local beliefs, Lord Vishnu had taken

'Mohini' form here to slay the monster, Bhasmasur. Due to this, the idol is decorated in Mohini form. However, the decoration—consisting of flowers, garlands, clothes, perfume and metal plating in certain parts, obscures the view of the devotee and conceals the inherent beauty of the idol.

Reflecting on the artistic creation of the idol, I pondered over the artist's perspective. When an artist creates artwork, they anticipate receiving compliments and credit for their creation. However, when an artist creates an idol that evolves into a deity worshipped by society, they relinquish control over it. It then becomes society's right to determine how the art should be presented. I contemplated the conflicting emotions an artist might experience—whether they would prefer to retain control and receive acclaim for their art or find greater satisfaction in seeing their creation attain a divine status through worship.

After taking darshan, we returned to explore the remaining pillars. Out of these, four are particularly renowned for their stunning carvings of women. One pillar features the craftsman skilfully using a chisel and hammer to carve the Mohini form, embodying feminine beauty. Two other pillars showcase Madanika, which we will discuss in detail later. The fourth pillar depicts King Vishnuvardhana's first queen, Queen Shantaladevi, providing insights into the time's societal dynamics.

Queen Shantaladevi, an expert in dance, is sculpted in a dance pose. The queen herself being an accomplished dancer is evidence of the fact that art and artists were greatly respected in those days. This is further confirmed by many important sculptures in the temple bearing the names of their sculptors, in recognition of their contributions. The status of women in society was evidently good. As a scholar of architecture, Queen Shantaladevi's inputs were considered while drawing up the design plans for the temple.

Women enjoyed considerable freedom, including the choice of their religious affiliation. Despite King Vishnuvardhana's conversion to Vaishnavism, Queen Shantaladevi continued to adhere to Jainism. Even though she continued to follow Jainism till the end, she served Lord Vishnu regularly in this temple by performing dances. She also took the initiative for and financed the Kappe Chennigaraya Temple in the temple premises. This temple is a miniature replica of the main temple and it is said that the builders built this grand temple using the replica for scale.

Like Queen Shantaladevi, the rest of King Vishnuvardhana's ministers also continued to follow Jainism. Many Jain temples were also built during that period. Like the Vishnu temple at Belur, the Hoysaleswara Shiva temple, rich in sculpture and art, was built for the Shaivites at Halebidu. In fact, the Hoysala-era temples have Shaivite, Shakta, Vaishnavite, Jain and Buddhist sculptures—proof of their secularism.

Queen Shantaladevi's commitment to her art earned her a special place in history. The government of Karnataka commemorates her lifelong dedication to dance by awarding the 'Shantala Natya Shri' award to individuals making significant contributions to the art of dance. Instituted in 1995, this annual award has a value of five lakh rupees.

THE BEAUTY OF SHALABHANJIKAS

As time passed, the influx of tourists increased, and the sun's heat intensified. The serene environment we encountered upon arrival had transformed into a lively one. The temple has a very good facility of trained and knowledgeable guides. It was a common sight to see a guide with an identity card around his neck, shining a torchlight on sculptures on the outer walls of the temple, with a group of tourists listening to him. After observing these activities, we proceeded to appreciate the artwork on the outer wall, starting from the east.

The celebrated sculpture that had escaped our initial notice while we were engrossed in darshan was now before us—the Darpan Sundari, often cited as an exemplary Indian sculpture. The sculpture is of a gorgeous woman looking at her face in the circular mirror in her hand, while bending her waist. Seeing her in person for the first time gave me a different kind of happiness of having seen something rare and incredible. These types of sculptures are known by many names such as 'Madanika', 'apsara', 'shalabhanjika or salabhanjika' and 'shilabalika'. They have an ancient history, tracing back to the eighth and ninth centuries. In the Puranas, they are revered as deities of motherhood and fertility, symbolizing prosperity and affluence. Associated with the birth of Buddha, the first use of the term 'shalabhanjika' is found in Buddhist scriptures.

Although the Darpana sculpture has received considerable attention, a total of forty-two similar sculptures can be found in the temple. These Madanika sculptures, standing on oval-shaped lotuses and framed by a carving of a sal tree arch, are a prominent feature. They are standing in tribhang mudra, with the body bent in three parts. The term 'Shalabhanjika' translates to the breaker of the branch of the sal tree, signifying her action in the sculpture. The sculptures, standing at two-and-a-half feet tall, depict Shalabhanjikas engaging in various activities. One gets to see the Shalabhanjika hunting, drying her hair after bathing, dancing, playing music, conducting shukbhashini with a parrot, markatamohini with a monkey pulling on her clothes and many more. These sculptures embody the ideals of female beauty and physique at the time.

The intricate details of the ornaments, fine pearls, rings, different hairstyles, and the details of feet and ankles in these sculptures seem almost impossible to be the work of human hands. Notably, in the main temple, there is a shukabashini shalbhanjika on one of the four pillars, where the bangle in her hand can be moved back and forth—a remarkable craftsmanship detail. A shalabhanjika in nritya mudra is an impressive sight: the manner in which the craftsman has captured the movement of her body, the swinging ornaments and her clothes is truly commendable!

Some scholars associate these shalabhanjikas with Queen Shantaladevi, suggesting that she served as the model for these sculptures, including Darpana. While it is challenging to ascertain the truth, Rekha Rao, a scholar of Indology, and a researcher in this field, hypothesizes this connection in her book *The Glory of Hoysala Queens*. She cites Chalukya king Someshvara-III's book *Abhilashitartha Chintamani*, linking the daily activities of Hoysala queens with those depicted in the sculptures. The fourth and fifth parts of this book describe the arts and hobbies that occupied the lives of women in the Hoysala and Chalukya dynasties. According to the descriptions, Rekha Rao contends that the daily activities of the queens align with those portrayed by the shalabhanjikas.

In Dr G.B. Deglurkar's book *Markandadev*, he delves into the significance of sursundaris, which are similar to the depictions of the shalabhanjikas. According to him, these sculptures convey a spiritual message to devotees, guiding them on the path to moksha, the ultimate goal of man in every religion. Attaining moksha involves renouncing five sensory aspects: words, touch, form, taste and smell. He contends that the depictions of these female figures are seen as teaching tools to impart wisdom on achieving salvation. For example, Darpana holding up the mirror symbolizes self-reflection, emphasizing that one must introspect, as no one else knows oneself better. Another sculpture featuring a woman trying to shake off a scorpion climbing on her lap represents the challenge of resisting temptation, with the scorpion's venom symbolizing desire. The monkey pulling on her clothes signifies a fickle and restless mind. The sculpture of a beauty playing with a ball symbolizes life. The ball touching the ground is symbolic of the soul entering the body to live life on earth, and the ball bouncing off of the ground is symbolic of the soul leaving the body and becoming one with God. This interpretation provides a fresh and thought-provoking perspective, considering these sculptures as teachings to steer clear of worldly temptations for spiritual attainment.

Observing the sculptures on the stone pillars outside the temple, we noticed that the sculptures in the temple are clearly divided into two types. The outer part of navrang mandapa is called jeevatma (earthly creatures) and the outer part of the sanctum sanctorum is called parmatma (gods). The sculptures outside the mandapa depict human life, while those outside the sanctum sanctorum portray deities, leading to the division known as Nara-Narayana (Man-God).

In the jeevatma section, the lowest sculpted panel depicts small, adorable elephants lazily clinging to each other. Above this panel, one can see layered sculpted panels depicting lions, men on horses, women engrossed in dancing and singing and some erotic sculptures. The net-like stone panel enclosing the mandapa has carvings of stories from the Puranas and the four pillars connected to the panel have sculptures of the shalabhanjikas.

Moving to the parmatma section, which resembles a densely packed country fair, eighty large-sized, exquisite sculptures of deities can be found. These include sculptures of Brahma, Vishnu, the Varaha avatar, the Narasimha avatar, the four avatars of Shiva, Mahishasuramardini, Durga, the Sun God with seven horses, Rati–Manmath and others. A particularly noteworthy sculpture depicts Ravana lifting Mount Kailasa, which is carved across an entire wall, showcasing the ingenuity of the sculptor in depicting all forms of life on the mountain. The sculpture depicts nine people on Mount Kailasa. The sculptures are in miniature form, and above them are Shiva–Parvati and Nandi. The appreciation for the talent and effort of these skilled artists grows as one moves forward and examines these idols.

OTHER TEMPLES IN THE COMPLEX

As previously mentioned, there are other sub-temples surrounding the main Chennakeshava Temple, each adorned with similar intricate sculptures. Among these, the Soumyanayaki Temple holds significance due to its peak resembling that of the Chennakeshava Temple. The Andal or Ranganayaki Temple on the north-west side is considered special as it is dedicated to the only female saint among the twelve Alvar saints. The sculptures on all these temples are magnificent.

However, the preservation of these temples faced challenges in the past. These temples, built in the twelfth century, had no security system till 1952. By that time, eighty-five sculptures from the outer wall of the main temple had been stolen and many sculptures were damaged in the attempt. The interlocked construction style of the temple, where the sculptures and sculpted panels were installed in the granite stone structure, contributed to the damage. First, the temple was built in granite stone and later, the sculptures and sculpted panels were installed in it. In 1952, the Archaeological Survey of

India was given custody of the temple and has been protecting it since. Regular chemical treatments are administered every ten years for the preservation of the temple.

While the Archaeological Survey of India has played a major role in maintaining this thousand-year-old temple, the reason it exists today is because of the intervention of the kings of Vijayanagara. Following the reign of Vir Ballala-II, Narasimha-II took the throne. Someshwara (1235 CE to 1253 CE) was the last glorious king of the Hoysala dynasty. After that, the kingdom faced division among the ruling sons. Temple construction ceased during this period. However, later, under the reign of Vir Ballala-III, who proved to be a powerful king, the two kingdoms were united. During his rule, the Hoysala kingdom faced threats from the cruel general Malik Kafur, serving under Alla-ud-din Khilji. The Khilji dynasty had conquered the neighbouring Hindu kingdoms of the Pandyas of Madurai, the Kakatiyas of Warangal and Kampil; and the Hoysala kingdom was the only kingdom they had not conquered. Despite attacks and invasions on neighbouring Hindu kingdoms, Vir Ballala-III fiercely defended his territory, preventing the Muslim invaders from conquering the Hoysala kingdom for three decades. His sacrifice on the battlefield while fighting the Madurai sultan in 1343 CE marked the end of an era.

The subsequent Hoysala king, Virupaksha-IV, could not safeguard the kingdom, leading to its eventual merger with the Vijayanagara kingdom, which emerged as the only Hindu kingdom in the south to repel the Muslim invasion. The Vijayanagara kings played a crucial role in maintaining and expanding the Chennakeshava Temple. The gopura, the Ranganayaki Temple, Soumyanayaki Temple, and other structures visible today were added during the reign of the Vijayanagara kings. It is due to the Hoysala kingdom falling into the hands of the Vijayanagara kings that these temples are still standing today.

The moment we had entered the temple premises, we were transported back in time and offered glimpses into the rich cultural and artistic heritage of ancient civilizations. The Chennakeshava Temple, with its intricate sculptures and historical significance, stands as a testament to the prosperous and culturally vibrant era of the Hoysala kings in the twelfth century. As you reflect on your visit, you carry with you not just memories but a deeper appreciation for the art, culture and philosophy that shaped that period. These temples indeed serve as priceless jewels, preserving the essence of Indian heritage for generations to come.

8

DELVING INTO THE MYSTERY OF THE SREE PADMANABHASWAMY TEMPLE

It is often said that the allure of the unknown captivates the human spirit. Being insatiably inquisitive from a young age, I have always found myself drawn to mysteries, driven to unravel their secrets. One such enigma that attracted me was the ancient temple of Sree Padmanabhaswamy. Unable to resist the urge to explore its mysteries, my husband and I planned a four-day trip to visit it during the Diwali holidays. Opting for this extended duration allowed us the opportunity to delve deep into the temple's history. Our intention was to visit repeatedly, soaking up as much knowledge as possible. To facilitate our exploration, we secured accommodations at a palace hotel in close proximity to the temple, granting us the freedom to visit as often as we liked.

The ancient Sree Padmanabhaswamy Temple, dedicated to Lord Vishnu, is located in the middle of Kerala's capital city, Thiruvananthapuram. The temple, a veritable cultural treasure, has been a hot topic due to its immense wealth. Revered by Vaishnavites, it was thrust into the limelight in 2011 due to an order by the Supreme Court of India. The order directed a detailed inventory of the temple's vaults and sparked widespread speculation about the ownership of this wealth, which is legally deemed to be the property of the deity Lord Padmanabhaswamy, i.e., Lord Vishnu himself. The order faced vehement opposition from the royal family of Travancore (who were handling the administration of the temple) and devotees.[20]

While the tremendous amount of wealth in the vaults accumulated over the centuries is certainly intriguing, I was

---

20 www.main.sci.gov.in/supremecourt/2011/10179/10179_2011 _32_1501_22898_Judgement_13-Jul-2020.pdf (p. 65).

personally more drawn by the cultural significance of this temple. During my research, I was overwhelmed by its rich history, artistic architecture, traditions and the myriad beliefs and myths surrounding the temple. I gleaned and collated information about the temple's heritage from as many sources as possible. After my research, I finally visited the incredible Sree Padmanabhaswamy Temple. In this account, I aim to convey the wealth of information I have gathered, beginning with a discussion on the temple's revered status, its architectural splendour, and the traditions and history that form an integral part of its identity.

While there is no accurate information about when the temple was constructed, references in ancient texts provide intriguing insights into its antiquity. According to the Shrimad Bhagavad Gita, during a tirth-yatra (pilgrimage), Balram visited Sree Padmanabhaswamy and bathed in the holy water of the Padmateertham. Several texts such as the Vishnu Purana, Padma Purana, Skanda Purana, Matsya Purana, Varaha Purana, Braamanda Purana and Brahma Purana, make a reference to the temple. Further attesting to its age, the works of ninth-century poet-saint Nammalwar (one of the twelve Vaishnavite saints of the Alwar tradition) also praise the temple. This lends credence to the belief that the temple predates the ninth century. Some historians such as Dr L.A. Ravi Verma postulate that the temple was built on the first day of the Kali Yuga, approximately 5,000 years ago.[21] While this view may be best disregarded, there is ample historical evidence to prove the ancient origins of the temple.

The renowned ancient scripture *Ananthasayana Mahatmya* narrates a fascinating tale about the consecration of the temple by a

---

21 https://trivandrum.nic.in/en/tourist-place/sree-padmanabha-swamy-temple/

Tulu Brahmin hermit named Divakaramuni. Divakarmuni, a devotee of Lord Vishnu, underwent rigorous penance until he was graced by Lord Vishnu's divine presence in the form of a child. Charmed by the boy, Divakaramuni requested him to stay. The boy agreed on the condition that he be treated with respect. The hermit agreed, and the two began living together. While the hermit was fond of the boy, the boy was very mischievous and would often cause trouble. One day, while the hermit was conducting pooja, the little boy defiled the pure shaligram (holy stone worshipped by Vaishnavites). Enraged, the hermit broke his promise and chastised the boy, who promptly vanished. While leaving, the boy revealed himself as Lord Vishnu and said, 'If you wish to meet me again, come to the Ananthakaadu.' Divakarmuni set out in search of Ananthakaadu. One day while searching, he came across a mother scolding her child, threatening to send the disobedient one to Ananthakaadu. He got directions from the woman and finally arrived at Ananthakaadu, located in a dense jungle near the sea. When he began praying to Lord Vishnu, a colossal tree collapsed before him and transformed into Lord Vishnu resting on the infinite serpent Adishesha. Divarkaramuni was overwhelmed and grateful that Lord Vishnu had graced him with his presence. However, since the divine form was gigantic, stretching across eight miles, the hermit prayed to Lord Vishnu to reduce his size to one which he could see in its entirety. The hermit's prayers were answered, and Lord Vishnu reduced his size. It is said that this was the place where the temple was consecrated.

An alternate version of this story replaces Divakaramuni with Namboodiri hermit Vilvamangalathu, a revered figure known for consecrating numerous ancient temples in south India. In this version, the hermit devotedly offered the deity pieces of mango, which he had taken from a nearby tree in a coconut shell as naivedya (sacred food offered to God). The practice endures to this day, where a naivedya of raw mango is offered to the deity in gold-plated cups. The similarities in the descriptions of Divakaramuni and Vilvamangalathu have led some to consider them as potentially the same person. Even today, the temple commissions Namboodiri Brahmin hermits to conduct the pushpanjali (offering of flowers) in the morning pooja. The temple's daily rituals commence with the first pooja at the early hour of 3.30 a.m., a serene and sacred time when devotees and tourists alike gather to witness this spiritual spectacle. For those eager to participate, the temple facilitates online bookings, allowing individuals to secure a time slot for the pooja by paying a nominal fee. My own experience, having made a reservation for the earliest pooja, remains etched in my memory—the tranquil sanctum sanctorum bathed in the warm glow of diyas (lamps), the crisp dawn air carrying the sweet fragrance of flowers, the resonant chanting of mantras and bells, and the collective devotion of worshippers chanting 'Govinda! Govinda!'

The temple is cited as the richest place of worship in the world. References to the temple's property in the form of land, money, gold coins, elephants, etc., as early as the fourteenth century, are recorded in the 'cadjan' leaf records. These invaluable records comprise approximately 3.5 lakh documents written in a blend of Malayalam and Tamil. They have been preserved in the state archive department, serving as a historical archive detailing social and political events from the fourteenth to the seventeenth century. Although the leaf records provide a wealth of information, the staggering riches stored within the temple's vaults find no mention in them. Before delving into the temple's wealth, it is crucial to understand the role of King Marthanda Varma, who, about 300 years ago in the eighteenth century, undertook the renovation that resulted in the magnificent temple we see today. The leaf records detail the administrative minutiae of this renovation.

Born in 1706, King Marthanda Varma, also known as Anizham Thirunal Marthanda Varma, ascended to the throne in 1729 and ruled until his death in 1758. The Varma dynasty were descendants of the mighty Chera dynasty in Kerala. Marthanda Varma succeeded to the throne following his uncle Rama Varma, in adherence to matrilineal customs. According to these customs, succession occurred through the king's sister's son, ensuring a balance of power between brothers and sisters.

When Marthanda Varma ascended to the throne, the kingdom was in turmoil—rampant corruption, a barren treasury, internal revolts and foreign invasions plagued the kingdom. The primary culprits were the Ettuveetil Pillamar (Lords of the Eight Houses)—corrupt nobles responsible for tax collection. They grew from ordinary landlords to powerful chiefs by exploiting their positions and misappropriating taxes. In order to maintain their power, they employed every method in the book—conspiring, fostering conflict within the royals, corruption, and even orchestrating assassinations. Having seen the antics of the Ettuveetil Pillamar, Marthanda Varma had gauged the looming threat they posed. He advised his uncle, King Rama Varma, to seek assistance from the Nayak dynasty of Madurai. Accordingly, battalions from the Nayaks' army were deployed for the security of the royal family. The Ettuveetil Pillamar realized that if Marthanda Varma succeeded to the throne, their stranglehold over the kingdom would be jeopardized.

In addition to internal challenges, various branches of the Chera dynasty posed external threats to the kingdom. The united Chera kingdom had split into smaller chiefdoms, one of which was the kingdom of Travancore. These small chiefdoms were constantly at war with each other. Despite the uncertain and distressing situation, King Marthanda Varma harboured ambitious dreams of uniting these smaller chiefdoms into a formidable empire. He decisively addressed the internal menace of the Ettuveetil Pillamar, dismantling their power structure. With a formidable army at his disposal, he shifted his focus to expanding his kingdom.

ARCHITECTURE AND SYMBOLISM AT THE TEMPLE

In terms of expanse, this temple sprawls across eight acres. It is said that the temple's architectural design is inspired by Hindu philosophy. The temple boasts nine doors, symbolizing the nine orifices of the human body, with the east-facing door being the primary entrance. Our visit to the temple began at this door during the early hours of dawn. The first sight that greets one is that of a vast padmateertham (holy tank) with robust stone steps, surrounded by eight small mandapas. While its ancient significance is rooted in the Shrimad Bhagavad Gita, which mentions it as the place where Balarama took a bath, the stone steps and mandapas were built during the reign of King Marthanda Varma. When we reached, the dawn was giving way to the morning. The bright sun rays gradually illuminated the deep blue sky, casting an orange hue. The padmateertham's reflective water mirrored its surroundings—the temple's gopura, nearby traditional tiny brick houses, swaying coconut trees and the picturesque sky. It was truly a sight to behold.

This tank has been considered an engineering marvel for centuries due to its abundant supply of sweet, fresh water. An ingenious system had been set up, whereby the water would be transported through underground pipelines from the dam on the Killi river about six kilometres away. After soaking in the beauty of this tank, we made our way towards the main entrance. We felt relieved that, unlike other religious sites, the perimeter of the temple was not teeming with hawkers. There were only a few shops lining the road that sold panchas (towels) and veshtis (cloth wrap for lower body, worn by men). These shops were thronged by tourists, in order to conform to the strict dress code of the temple. The temple administration is quite rigid in its implementation of the temple dress code rules, which mandates that devotees wear sari, skirt, panchas or veshtis and does not permit pants, salwars, slacks, etc. Most tourists were unaware of this dress code and were scrambling to purchase the clothes that would allow them to enter. Fortunately, being aware of the dress code, we were appropriately attired and hastened towards the entrance.

The foundation for the gopura was laid in 1566 on the east entrance and the construction of the gopura was completed during the reign of King Marthanda Varma. The grand seven-tiered gopura, adorned with ornate sculptures and window-like openings in the centre of each tier, dominated the skyline. The entrance to the temple and the window-like openings are aligned vertically, in a straight line. This architectural marvel, standing approximately thirty-five metres high, is considered a brilliant example of the Dravidian style of architecture, popular in south India.

The peak of the gopura is adorned with seven golden kalash (urns), which are considered to be symbols of the seven lokas (worlds) as mentioned in the Vishnu Purana: Atal, Vital, Sutal, Rasatal, Talatal, Mahatal and Patal. The first tier of the gopura is decorated with sculptures of the ten avatars of Lord Vishnu (Matsya, Kurma, Varaha, Narasimha, Vaman, Shri Ram, Shri Krishna, Parashurama, Buddha and Kalki). The gopura is considered a scientific wonder due to a rare spectacle that unfolds twice a year on the equinox occurring on 20 March and 23 September. During these days, the sun aligns perfectly to pass through all the window-like openings from top to bottom. The gopura's construction involved precise geometrical techniques to ensure this captivating spectacle. Each year, devotees and curious onlookers gather to witness the sun's passage through these openings. This temple, a product of the matrimony of imagination, skills and scientific knowledge, leaves visitors stunned.

After a thorough security check, we were granted entry into the temple. Upon entering, we were first greeted by the spacious rectangular path for circumambulation. The path is marked by tall, sculpted monolithic pillars. Numbering 365 in total, these pillars symbolize the days in a year. Despite the temple deity being Lord Vishnu, many pillars feature sculptures of Shivalingas. Each pillar on the path showcases a sculpture of a woman holding a hollow diya. On festive occasions, these lamps are filled with oil and illuminated, creating a mesmerizing sight as the circumambulation path is bathed in the glow of 365 diyas. The circumambulation path and pillars were built during the reign of King Marthanda Varma. It is said that the construction was completed in merely six months with the aid of 4,000 sculptors, 6,000 labourers and 100 elephants. The surprisingly swift pace of the construction reflects the king's immense devotion towards the Lord and the prosperity of the kingdom.

The prosperity of the kingdom was a result of King Marthanda Varma's efforts to revive the kingdom after it had been ravaged by the exploits of the Ettuveetil Pillamar. As discussed earlier, upon assuming the throne, the king defeated the Ettuveetil Pillamar. However, in order to defeat the faction, a critical event had to occur. One of the festivals observed by the Padmanabhaswamy Temple is the festival of Arattu, during which there is a ritual involving bathing the idols of the temple deities by dipping them in a water body. There is a huge procession for carrying the idol to the water body and back to the temple, in which members of the royal family also participate. People attend the procession donning various colourful costumes, allowing the king to easily attend the festival in disguise. Taking advantage of the access to the king, a conspiracy was hatched to assassinate King Marthanda Varma. Fortunately, the king learnt of the conspiracy through his informants in advance, leading to the apprehension and execution of the conspirators. This procession takes place, even today, on the same five-kilometre path used for centuries. A section of the path crosses an international airport and, interestingly, the airport remains closed on the day of the festival for five whole hours until the procession has crossed the runway, in honour of the tradition. It is the first airport in the world that is closed twice in a year for a festival procession.

After the king defeated the Ettuveetil Pillamar, no one dared to oppose him. In place of the Ettuveetil Pillamar, King Marthanda Varma deputed trustworthy and qualified persons to manage tax collection. This move stabilized the kingdom, bringing order to the chaos. King Marthanda Varma introduced groundbreaking economic policies, being the first king of Travancore to initiate an economic budget. The budget prioritized religion through the construction of temples and national security through the fortification of the army. He was also the first to impose land taxes proportional to the size of the land. Realizing the importance of commerce and ocean trade, he took the necessary steps to capitalize on it. The implementation of the new policies introduced by the king swiftly made the kingdom prosperous and filled up the coffers of the treasury.

As we strolled along the circumambulation path, the enchanting strains of a classical music performance reached our ears from the mandapa on our right. Since it was the auspicious dawn of Diwali, a singer was devoting his music to Lord Vishnu. A chance to perform here is highly coveted and commands great respect. We settled in for some time to enjoy the music.

The temple is surrounded by eleven mandapas, each serving various purposes such as pooja, hymn chanting, meditation and musical performances. Some of the mandapas have intricately carved wooden roofs. Of these eleven mandapas, the Kulshekhar mandapa stands out with its beautifully carved columns depicting stories from the Puranas, and its twenty-eight pillars. It is also known as Saptaswara mandapa (mandapa of seven musical notes) since one can hear seven musical notes by striking the four corner pillars. However, this mandapa is not open to the public.

Approaching the main shrine, our attention was captured by the flagpole made of teak wood and encased in gold transported by sea from Tamil Nadu. The flagpole is surrounded by pillars adorned with finely carved sculptures of Hindu deities. To the left of the main temple entrance, a sculpture of the fierce Chamunda Devi, with a skeleton for her body and a necklace of skulls, commands attention. Grand sculptures of Garuda and Hanuman, both with folded hands, also flank the entrance. Similar to the Chennakeshwara Temple built by the Hoysala dynasty in Karnataka, intricately carved sculptures of Rati and Kamadev stand on either side of the entrance. This pair, a symbolic representation of lust, placed opposite to each other, conveys an implicit message to visitors to set aside worldly desires upon entering the sacred premises. Since cameras and mobile phones are restricted in this area, the only way to capture these exquisite sculptures is to etch them into one's memory.

While we were immersed in the intricate sculptures, the line for darshan continued to grow longer. The popularity of this temple, combined with specific visiting hours, always results in long queues. Throughout our four-day visit, whether day or night, we found ourselves standing in line each time. An option to bypass the line is available by paying an additional fee at the ticket counter. However, choosing not to pay the extra fee allows ample time to appreciate the artistic interiors and craftsmanship of the temple. We joined the queue, adorned in panchas and veshtis.

Following the line, we reached the small temple dedicated to the fierce Narasimha. After visiting this temple, we crossed its small door and entered the main temple. Adjacent to the sanctum sanctorum, there is a square-shaped mandapa housing the idol of Padmanabhaswamy, a depiction of Lord Vishnu. The roof of the mandapa is made of monolithic granite and is 2.5 feet in width and twenty feet long. The sculpted pillars of the mandapa are also made of granite. Both the roof and the pillars of the mandapa are gold-plated. The eighteen-foot idol of Padmanabhaswamy in the sanctum sanctorum is breathtaking. This enchanting idol depicts Lord Vishnu in Anantha Shayana (eternal yogic sleep) on the serpent god Adishesha. The right hand of Lord Vishnu hovers over the Shivalinga. The hoods formed by the five heads of Adishesha fan out and form a roof over the head of Lord Vishnu and a padma (lotus) emerges from the nabhi (navel) of Lord Vishnu. The four-headed Lord Brahma sits atop the lotus.

This idol is significant for multiple reasons. The idol depicts the big three of Hinduism—Brahma (the Creator), Vishnu (the Preserver) and Shiva (the Destroyer)—disregarding the rigid distinction traditionally followed in Vaishnavite and Shaivite temples. The manner in which one can see the grand idol brings us back to the story of the consecration of the temple. It is said that when the saint requested the Lord to shrink in size, his view was still obstructed by Iluppai trees and he saw the Lord in three parts: thirumukham (head), thiruvudal (navel) and thrippadam (feet). Even today, visitors can see the idol through three doors. The first door affords a view of the heads of the snake and the face of Lord Vishnu, his right hand and the Shivalinga. The second door shows the lotus flower emerging from the navel and Lord Brahma on it. The third door shows the feet of Lord Vishnu. These three doors are considered to be reflective of the three stages of life, viz., childhood, youth and old age. The five hoods of Adishesha are considered to be symbols of the five elements: fire, air, earth, water and the sky; and the three curves formed by the curling serpent are considered symbols of the three gunas (qualities of energy): sattva (peace and harmony), rajas (activity and passion) and tamas (darkness and chaos).

The idol is studded with 12,008 shaligrams (variety of stone collected from the riverbed of the Gandaki, considered a non-anthropomorphic representation of Lord Vishnu) brought here during the reign of King Marthanda Varma from the Gandaki river, situated in modern-day Nepal. It is said that twelve shaligrams possess the piousness of one tirtha-kshetra (pilgrimage site). Devotees, therefore, believe that this idol a thousand times as sacred as one tirtha-kshetra. Seeing the beautiful idol, illuminated by an oil lamp that never goes out, brings tranquility to the mind. We then visited the adjoining kshetrapal (Hindu guardian deity of consecrated land or farmland) and Shri Krishna temple. While walking out of the temple on the circumambulation path, we heard the melodious voice of famous Carnatic classical musician Subbulakshmi singing the 'Vishnu Sahasranam' (a Sanskrit hymn). It left us speechless and our minds felt completely at peace.

THE HIDDEN WEALTH

Now, let us learn about the wealth housed in this temple. Even before the Supreme Court pronounced its decision in 2011, the temple's affluence was common knowledge. However, the figures disclosed after the inventory drew the world's attention to this temple. The value of the wealth was measured at rupees 10,00,00,00,00,000 (rupees one lakh crore), a figure that becomes infinitely higher after considering the antique value of the wealth. To understand the source of this wealth, we need to rewind to the era of King Marthanda Varma. In the fifteenth century, present-day Kerala was divided into numerous small and fragmented chiefdoms. The arrival of Europeans for trade further complicated the scenario. The French tried to exert control over north Kerala; meanwhile, the British built forts at Malabar and Travancore. These foreigners were trying to capitalize on the conflict between the small chiefdoms and were exerting control by offering security and better trade relations.

The Dutch East India Company, which ruled over Indonesia for over two centuries, equipped with modern weaponry and warships, emerged as the aggressor. The company had taken over the major kingdoms of Kerala viz. Calicut and Kochi. The Dutch, as well as King Marthanda Varma, were well aware that these territories were crucial for ocean trade. King Marthanda Varma strategically took over Port Kayamkulam in 1734 and then set his sights on the Port of Kollam. This move alarmed the Dutch. At the time, King Marthanda Varma was already on an expansion spree, conquering the small neighbouring chiefdoms. In a short period, he had taken control of the long stretch from Kanyakumari to Kochi. Since their monopoly contracts with these small chiefdoms (now vassals of the kingdom of Travancore) were not being honoured and severely impacting their trade, the Dutch put forth their business terms to King Marthanda Varma and threatened to start a war if he did not accept them. Unfazed by their ultimatum, the king defiantly stated that Travancore was even contemplating invading Europe. Enraged, the Dutch declared war. The strong and well-equipped Dutch army forced the king to retreat.

After this victory, under the leadership of skilled military strategist Captain De Lannoy, the Dutch arrived at the Port of Colachel. They began to prepare for their attack on Padmanabhapuram, the capital of Travancore. King Marthanda Varma was fully prepared for the attack. A hostile war took place between the Dutch and Travancore at Colachel in which the Dutch were sorely defeated. Being the brilliant strategist that he was, King Marthanda Varma diplomatically made an offer to the Dutch and traded black pepper in exchange for their modern weaponry. The war made King Marthanda Varma the first Indian ruler to defeat the Europeans. After this war, some Dutch soldiers, comprising Captain De Lannoy and twenty-three European officers, were imprisoned. Later, King Marthanda Varma magnanimously offered to let these prisoners join the Travancore army, proving his long-sightedness. The king also recognized the value of Captain De Lannoy and invited him to revolutionize and modernize the army of Travancore, which he accepted.

Captain De Lannoy's contributions transformed the Travancore army and fortified its defences. He went on to serve the Travancore army for thirty-seven years and rose to the rank of 'valia kapitaan' (commander-in-chief). He served in the army until his death and was buried at the Udayagiri Fort. When India became independent from the British Empire in 1947, the Travancore army was subsumed into the Indian Army and became the 9th battalion of the Madras Regiment. Every year on 31 July, this battalion celebrates the victory of Travancore in the Colachel war by visiting the monument at Colachel built in honour of this victory.

Following this victory, King Marthanda Varma gradually brought all of south India and the spice trade under his control, amassing immense wealth, which ended up enriching the temple. From the fourteenth century, the Padmanabhaswamy Temple had steadily accumulated riches in its coffers; however, in 1749, it received a significant inflow of wealth. This notable event occurred when the king performed the 'Thripatti Danam' ritual. By way of this ritual, this brilliant, ambitious king who had amassed wealth on his own strength, performed the greatest act of devotion possible for a king: he donated his entire kingdom and all its wealth to Lord Padmanabhaswamy and declared that he would live the rest of his life as a vassal of the deity and merely oversee the kingdom on the Lord's behalf. During the ritual, he surrendered his crown and his sword at the feet of the Lord. His decision was respected and all his descendants including King Balarama Varma (1912–91) continued as vassals of the deity.

While King Marthanda Varma significantly contributed to the temple's wealth, donations from devotees and taxes collected from the kingdom also added to it. The tradition of donating the prince's weight in gold upon reaching adulthood further increased the gold reserves. It is believed that the temple's wealth has been accumulating since the period of the Venadu dynasty. This might explain why the vaults are not mentioned in the leaf records maintained from the fourteenth to the seventeenth century. The kings, over the centuries, may have deposited the wealth in the vaults for security reasons.

Several legends, one of which claims that anyone touching the wealth will die soon after, are associated with the wealth, which may be the reason it is well-preserved. Until India attained Independence,

King Marthanda Varma and his descendants maintained tight control over the kingdom of Travancore and the temple administration. Thereafter, King Marthanda Varma's descendants continued to be trustees of the Padmanabhaswamy Temple, a position they hold even today. In July 2020, the Indian Supreme Court recognized the right of the titular King of Travancore to act as the trustee of the temple. The titular king is honoured by allowing him to conduct pooja on special occasions, and a daily time slot is reserved for the king to perform pooja, during which devotees are not allowed to enter the main temple.

In 2007, a young lawyer named Ananda Padmanabhan filed a suit before a lower court in Trivandrum on behalf of two devotees alleging maladministration of the temple's wealth by the trustees.[22] The lawyer, being a devotee of Padmanabhaswamy, would regularly visit the temple. During his daily visits, he grew concerned about the lack of adequate security for the temple's riches, the rumours of parts of the wealth disappearing, and the absence of any written record inventorying the wealth. The Trivandrum lower court allowed the suit and directed the state to take control of the temple and its possessions. The Kerala High Court upheld this decision in 2011, further directing the state to constitute a trust for the administration of the temple. A special leave petition was filed before the Supreme Court challenging the Kerala High Court decision. In 2011, the Supreme Court passed an interim order in the special leave petition directing inventory of all the items in the vaults, as mentioned earlier. The incredible amount of wealth, the fact that it was considered to be owned by Lord Vishnu and the deadly myths associated with

---

22 https://blog.ipleaders.in/critical-analysis-on-sree-padmanabhaswamy-temple-case/

the opening of the vaults resulted in the interim order being hotly debated.

Following the Supreme Court's directions, six out of the eight known vaults (vaults 'A', 'B', 'C', 'D', 'E', 'F', 'G', and 'H') were opened and inventoried by a seven-member committee constituted by the Supreme Court. The committee found gold, silver, gems, other precious stones in the form of jewellery and idols, coins from various countries and empires, as well as other artefacts. While vaults 'C', 'D', 'E' and 'F' were opened from time to time by the main priest of the temple, Vault 'B' was said to be unopened for centuries. Despite the court directions, Vault 'B' could not be opened due to its complex opening mechanism.

There were myths associated with Vault 'B', such as there being an engraved image of two cobras on the door and a belief that opening it would cause a catastrophic flood destroying the world. There was vehement opposition to the opening of this vault, both by members of the royal family and by devotees. Unfortunately, fifteen days post the opening of the vaults, T.P. Sundararajan, the seventy-year-old senior lawyer arguing the matter on behalf of the two devotees, and who was also one of the observers when the vault was opened, passed away. T.P. Sundararajan's death reinforced the myth of the curse that would befall a person who would dare to touch the temple's wealth in the minds of the devotees who were opposed to the temple administration being handed over to the state.[23]

In August 2011, the temple administration organized a ritual called 'Devaprashnam' to seek the opinion of the gods in relation

---

23 www.thehindu.com/news/national/kerala/in-numbers-the-story-behind-sree-padmanabhaswamy-temple-vaults/article19251538.ece

to the opening of Vault 'B'. The four-day ritual was conducted by six renowned astrologers. They concluded that the gods opposed the opening of the vault, warning that events of deadly destruction would follow if it were to be opened. The Supreme Court criticized the temple administration for conducting such a ritual while the matter was sub judice. There are earlier references to the attempts to open these vaults as well. In a 1933 guidebook titled *Travancore: A Guide Book for the Visitor* by Emily Gilchrist Hatch, there is a reference to an unsuccessful attempt in 1908 to open the vaults, which failed due to an apparent infestation of cobras. However, there are references to the vaults being successfully opened on 6 December 1931.

After the inventory of the vaults, the Kerala state government has been charged with ensuring the security of the vaults with the assistance of central security agencies. Devotees are subjected to stringent security checks before entering the temple. Despite only gaining prominence from 2007 onwards due to the court case, millions of devotees have been visiting the Padmanabhaswamy Temple for years. Even today, Hindu devotees (only Hindus are allowed entry to the temple) continue to line up for a glimpse of the great Lord Vishnu, following the strict dress code of the temple. Lord Vishnu is also known as 'Bhagwan'. The meaning of 'Bhag' is explained in the Vishnu Purana as one possessing the six qualities of majesty, knowledge, abstinence, wealth, success and the power to sustain the world. One can say the greatness of this Bhagwan Lord Vishnu brings millions of devotees to the doors of the Padmanabhaswamy Temple.

GLOSSARY

Adhishtan	Base of a temple structure
Adishesha	Serpentine demigod (naga) and king of the serpents
Aghor–Agnitattva	A form inspired by fire, a symbol of *ichha shakti* or will power
Agni	Hindu god of fire
Airavata	Divine white elephant and vehicle of Indra who was born out of the churning of the sea
Anantha Shayana	Eternal yogic sleep
Annapurna	A manifestation of Parvati, known as the Hindu goddess of food and nourishment.
Antaral	Space between the mandapa and the sanctum sanctorum
Apsara	Mythical celestial nymphs in Hindu and Buddhist traditions

Ardha mandapa	Half-open hall
Ardhanarinateshwar	Form of Shiva combined with his consort Parvati, depicted as half-male and half-female, equally split down the middle
Ashta Dikpalas	Group of eight deities ruling over the eight quarters of the Universe
Atmalinga	Representation of the soul of Shiva
Avasthitha	Forms inspired by elements which make the Universe
Avatar	Incarnation
Bali peetham	Small platform for offering sacrifice
Bhairav	Fierce avatar of Shiva
Bharatanatyam	Classical Indian dance form that originated in Tamil Nadu
Bhudevi	Hindu goddess who represents the earth, fertility, sustenance and nurturing
Bhumi	Another name for Bhudevi
Brahma	Major Hindu deity in the Hindu trinity, associated with creation
Chaitya	Shrine
Chakra	Circular throwing weapon
Chamunda	Hindu goddess of war and epidemics, famines, and other disasters
Chandra	Hindu moon god
Chaupar	Strategic board game played in India
Dakshinamurti	An incarnation of Shiva, the supreme god of knowledge

GLOSSARY

Damaru	Small two-headed drum associated with Shiva
Darshan	Viewing the garbhagriha of the temple, which hosts the idol of God
Deepa stambha	Lamp pillar
Dhamma	Central belief in Buddhism which means 'to uphold'
Dhanvantri	The physician of the gods in Hindu mythology
Dharma	Religious and moral law governing individual conduct
Dhvajastambha	Flagstaff
Diya	Lamp
Durga	Hindu goddess of power, strength and protection
Dwarapalas	Guardians of the entrance to a temple
Gada	Mallet or a blunt mace
Gajacharama	Elephant skin
Gajalakshmi	A form of the goddess Lakshmi depicted with elephants
Ganas or Shivaganas	Attendants or followers of Shiva
Ganesh	One of the most-worshipped Hindu deities, characterized by his elephant head; he is the remover of obstacles and bringer of good luck
Garbhagriha	The sanctum sanctorum, the innermost chamber of a Hindu temple where the deity resides

Garuda	Hindu deity, king of the birds, mount of Vishnu
Gathas	Verses
Gopuras	Entrance gateways
Gunas	Qualities of energy in Hinduism, the three gunas are sattva (peace and harmony), rajas (activity and passion) and tamas (darkness and chaos)
Guru	Teacher
Hanuman	Hindu deity, revered as a divine vanara (monkey), and a devoted companion of the Ram (an incarnation of Vishnu)
Harihara	Dual representation of Vishnu (Hari) and Shiva (Hara)
Hiranyakashipuvadh	The depiction of the slaying of the asura Hiranyakashipu
Hom-havan	Offerings made to a sacred fire
Idli	South Indian rice cake cooked using steam
Indra	King of the gods, Hindu god of weather
Ishaan	A Hindu god and the guardian of the northeast direction
Ishaan-Akaashtattva	A form inspired by the sky, a symbol of *atindriya shakti* or transcendental power
Jagati	Raised platform surrounding the temple
Janva	Sacred thread
Jyotirlinga	A devotional representation of Shiva as a pillar of light
Kaaliyamardan	Krishna's subduing of the serpent Kaliya

Kalaari or Kalantak	Shiva as the conqueror of time and death
Kalash	Urn
Kali	Hindu goddess of time, change, creation, power, destruction and death
Kalyanasundara	Its literal meaning is 'beautiful wedding', an iconographical depiction of the wedding of the Hindu deities Shiva and Parvati
Kamandalu	Small, globular or ovoid water pot used by ascetics to carry drinking water and for ritual ablutions
Kamadeva	Hindu god of love and desire
Kanchanmruga	The illusional golden deer from the Ramayana
Kartikeya	Son of Shiva and Parvati, a significant deity in Hinduism
Khadga	Sword
Krishna	The eighth avatar or incarnation of Vishnu
Kshetrapal	Hindu guardian deity of consecrated land or farmland
Kshira sagara	Ocean of milk in Hindu cosmology
Kuber	Hindu god of wealth
Kumbhak	A spherical summit
Kunda	Pond
Lakshmi	Hindu goddess of wealth and prosperity
Leni	Marathi word for cave
Linga	An abstract representation of Shiva

Lingodbhava	Iconic representation of Shiva emerging out of jyotirlinga, the pillar of light
Lokas	Realms of existence in Hinduism
Maha mandapa	Great gathering hall
Mahabharata	One of the two major Smriti texts and Sanskrit epics of ancient India, revered in Hinduism
Mahayana	One of the branches of Buddhism
Maheshwar	A name of Shiva
Mahishasurmardini	A form of Durga, also known as Kali, as the slayer of the buffalo demon Mahishasura
Makara torana	Decorative arches with crocodile motifs
Mandapa	A pillared outdoor hall or pavilion for public rituals in Hindu, Jain and Buddhist temples
Manmanth	Another name for Kamadeva
Mohini	Female avatar of Vishnu as the Hindu goddess of enchantment
Moksha	Freedom from the cycle of birth and death
Mount Kailasa	Sacred mountain, abode of Shiva
Mudras or nritya mudras	Hand gestures or pure dance mudras used in Indian classical dance performances
Mukha mandapa	Pavilion in front of the doorway of the temple
Nagaraja	A serpent king in Hindu mythology
Naivedya	Sacred food offered to God
Nandi	The sacred bull and vehicle of Shiva

GLOSSARY

Nandi mandapa	A hall or pavilion dedicated to the sacred bull Nandi
Narasimha	Avatar of Vishnu as a half-man, half-lion
Nataraj or Nrityashiva	A form of Shiva as the cosmic dancer
Navas	A vow to a god often involving the promise of an offering in return for a request granted
Nayanars	Group of sixty-three Tamil Hindu saints who lived during the sixth to eighth centuries CE, who were devoted to Shiva
Nirutti	One of the eight dikpalas (guardians of directions)
Padmasana	Lotus pose, a cross-legged sitting meditation pose from ancient India
Padmateertham	Holy tank
Panchas	Towels
Panigrahan	Vedic marriage ritual where the groom takes the bride's hand
Parivar devatas	Family deities
Parvati	Hindu goddess of power, nourishment, devotion, motherhood, fertility and harmony; wife of Shiva
Pashupatastra	Celestial missile
Patal	The underworld as per Hindu cosmology
Pooja	Hindu act of worship or propitiation
Puranas	Genre of ancient Indian literature containing mythological stories
Pushpanjali	Offering of flowers to God

Ramayana	One of the two major Smriti texts and Sanskrit epics of ancient India, revered in Hinduism
Rangamahal	A mandapa or hall, often used for performances or gatherings
Rati	Hindu goddess of love, lust, passion and sexual pleasure
Ravana	Ancient mythological king of the island of Lanka, chief antagonist in the Hindu epic Ramayana
Rudrakshamala	Prayer beads
Rudras	Avatars of Shiva
Sadyojaat–Prithvitattva	A form inspired by earth, a symbol of *kriya shakti* or driving force
Salwars	Cloth worn from the waist to the ankles, covering both legs separately
Samants	Feudatories
Sambar	South Indian dish consisting of lentils and vegetables cooked with tamarind
Samudra manthana	Major episode in Hinduism involving the churning of the sea
Saptamatrikas	Seven mother goddesses associated with various deities
Saptaswari or Saptaswara	Seven musical notes
Sari	Garment worn by Hindu women, consisting of a long piece of cotton or silk wrapped around the body with one end draped over the head or over one shoulder

GLOSSARY

Shaivism	Major denomination of Hinduism that worships Shiva
Shaivites	Devotees of Shiva who consider him as the Supreme Being
Shaligram	Holy stone considered a non-anthropomorphic representation of Vishnu worshipped by Vaishnavites
Sharabheshwar	Depiction of Shiva as a part-lion, part-bird beast
Sheshashayi Vishnu	Vishnu resting on the serpent Shesha
Shikhara	The rising tower or spire above the sanctum sanctorum of a Hindu temple
Shiva	A principal deity in Hinduism, known as the god of destruction and regeneration
Shivalinga	A symbolic representation of Shiva
Shloka	A thirty-two-syllable verse commonly used in classical Sanskrit literature
Shridevi	Another name for Lakshmi
Soma	Hindu deity who supervises religious sacrifices
Sthambha	Pillar
Stupa	Mound-shaped or hemispherical structure that is a significant part of Buddhist architecture
Subhashitas	Sanskrit epigrammatic poems
Surya	Hindu sun god
Suryavanshi	Descendants of Surya
Tandava	Divine dance performed by Shiva

Tarakasura	A powerful asura, i.e., demon in Hindu mythology
Tatpurush–Vayutattva	A form inspired by air, a symbol of *pran shakti* or life force
Theravada	One of the branches of Buddhism
Tirtha-kshetra	Sites of pilgrimage
Tirtha-yatra	Pilgrimage
Torana	Ornamental gateway
Tribhang mudra	Standing body position or stance used in traditional Indian art and Indian classical dance forms where the body bends in one direction at the knees, the other direction at the hips and then the other again at the shoulders and neck
Trishul	Trident, primary weapon of Shiva
Trivikrama	Another name for Vishnu, often associated with his cosmic stride
Upapeetha	The lower tier of the basement of a temple
Uthavashilpa	Bas-relief sculptures
Vaamdeva–Jalatattva	A form inspired by water, a symbol of *dnyana shakti* or the power of knowledge
Vada	Indian dish in which ground pulses are shaped into a ball and deep-fried
Vahana	Vehicle or mount
Vaishnavism	A major denomination of Hinduism that worships Vishnu
Vaishnavite	Devotees of Vishnu who consider him as the Supreme Being

Varaha avatar	Incarnation of Vishnu as a boar
Varshavas	Rainy months during which Buddhist monks take shelter in one place
Varun	Hindu god associated with the sky, oceans and water
Vastra	Cloth
Vasuki	Second king of snakes, often depicted coiled around the neck of Shiva
Veena	Chordophone instrument from the Indian subcontinent
Veshtis	Cloth wrap for the lower body, worn by men
Vimana	The tower above the sanctum sanctorum in a Hindu temple
Virbhadra	A fierce form of Shiva
Vishnu	A principal deity in Hinduism, known as the preserver of the universe
Vishnu sahasranam	A Sanskrit hymn
Yagna or Yajna	Fire ritual during which sacrificial offerings are made
Yajnashala	A hall used for performing rituals or ceremonies
Yamaraj	Hindu god of death
Yamatirtham	A pilgrimage site associated with Yama

ACKNOWLEDGEMENTS

This book has been a journey of love, dedication, and the unwavering support of many wonderful individuals. A thousand thanks to:

My husband, Vinod, for being a source of unconditional support in my life. You've made the impossible, possible. This book would not exist without you.

My lovely daughters, Aboli and Anuli, you have both expanded my horizons and awakened a deeper sense of self-awareness in me. Your love and encouragement mean the world.

A very special thanks in particular to Aboli. This book, in its English form, owes its existence to your tireless efforts. You found time amidst your studies and busy schedule to translate this book with immense dedication, out of your love for me. You have my love and blessings always.

Neelima Kulkarni of Rajendra Prakashan, thank you for treating my dream project as yours and for bringing it to life in the Marathi language. Your belief in this work has been crucial to its success.

Dr G.B. Deglurkar, I am deeply grateful for your invaluable guidance and for graciously writing the foreword. Your insights have added immense value to this book.

Lipika Bhushan and the HarperCollins team, your hard work and dedication have ensured that this book reaches as many people as possible. I am truly thankful for your efforts.

Finally, I want to express my heartfelt gratitude to the many readers who embraced the Marathi edition of this book with great enthusiasm. Your desire to see this work translated into English has been a driving force, and I am deeply appreciative of your support.

Thank you all for making this journey possible.

HarperCollins *Publishers* India

At HarperCollins India, we believe in telling the best stories and finding the widest readership for our books in every format possible. We started publishing in 1992; a great deal has changed since then, but what has remained constant is the passion with which our authors write their books, the love with which readers receive them, and the sheer joy and excitement that we as publishers feel in being a part of the publishing process.

Over the years, we've had the pleasure of publishing some of the finest writing from the subcontinent and around the world, including several award-winning titles and some of the biggest bestsellers in India's publishing history. But nothing has meant more to us than the fact that millions of people have read the books we published, and that somewhere, a book of ours might have made a difference.

As we look to the future, we go back to that one word—a word which has been a driving force for us all these years.

Read.